The 500 Hidden Secrets of

ROME

INTRODUCTION

It's easy to get stuck with the idea of Rome as the Eternal City, an extraordinary yet immutable place where change is difficult to come about, and whose fame rests on its past. This book invites you to wander and wonder beyond the surface and off the beaten path, look deeper, discover different sides of this charming and lively capital, and, from time to time, to venture away from the most crowded areas of the city centre.

The main objective of this publication is to guide the reader to the places that are not usually included in tourist guides, and to point out details that are generally overlooked. Like the other 'Colosseum', the Amphitheatre Castrense, which now hosts a gorgeous Cistercian garden whose contemporary gate was designed by artist Jannis Kounellis.

At the same time it also lists cool places to discover and buy contemporary crafts, explore lesser-known bookstores, libraries, and music stores, and turn the shopping experience into a pleasant surprise. An example? The Gatsby Cafè, where you can buy a designer hat, while sipping on a cocktail, in a 1950s-inspired atmosphere.

The list is far from being complete and all-encompassing. Rather, it is the fruit of a personal selection, as if it were a private art collection, so the authors' tastes have played a strong influence on the choices. In keeping with the spirit of the publication, they picked those sites which are more off the radar, or introduce an element of novelty in the Roman panorama: they offer some cues for those with a curious eye.

HOW TO
USE THIS BOOK?

———————————

This guide lists 500 things you need to know about Rome in 100 different categories. Most of these are places to visit, with practical information like the address and sometimes opening hours or info on making reservations. Others are bits of information that help you get to know the city and its people. The purpose of this guide is to inspire you to explore the city, but it doesn't cover every aspect from A to Z.

The places in this guide are given an address, including the neighbourhood (for example 'Trastevere and Gianicolo' or 'East Rome'), and a number. The neighbourhood and number allow you to find the places on the maps at the beginning of the book: first look for the map of the corresponding neighbourhood, then look for the right number. A word of caution however: these maps are not detailed enough to allow you to find specific locations in the city. They are included to give you a sense of where places are, and whether they are close by other places of interest. You can obtain an excellent map from any tourist office or in most hotels. Or the addresses can be located on a smartphone.

Please also bear in mind that cities change all the time. The chef who hits a high note one day may be uninspiring on the day you happen to visit. The bar considered one of the 5 best places to sip on an *aperitivo* might be empty on the night you're there. This is obviously a highly personal selection. You might not always agree with it. If you want to leave a comment, recommend a bar or reveal your favourite secret place, please visit the website *the500hiddensecrets.com* – you'll also find free tips and the latest news about the series there – or follow *@500hiddensecrets* on Instagram or Facebook and leave a comment.

THE AUTHORS

Christopher Livesay is a TV correspondent for CBS News. Based in Rome, he's covered Italy for more than a decade, as well as other countries around the world, from the Arctic to the Sahara. He holds bachelor's degrees in art history and Italian from Arizona State University, and a master's from the Columbia University Graduate School of Journalism. He first came to Italy for adventure, but stayed for love – both of the country and the co-author.

Luisa Grigoletto is a travel expert based in Rome, planning bespoke off-the-beaten-path trips for Trufflepig, a Canadian travel company. *Condé Nast Traveler* has named her a Top Travel Specialist for Italy. She has extensive experience as a travel, art, and photography writer, contributing to such publications as *Lonely Planet, Time Out, Frieze,* and *AfterImage.*

Luisa and Christopher wrote this book after years of learning about Rome the hard way. The Eternal City is not a user-friendly city. They made all the mistakes, waited in all the wrong lines, and ate at all the tourist traps before they got to the secret gems that are in this book, and that make this city such an extraordinary privilege to live in, and to visit.

They are infinitely grateful to their friends and colleagues who helped them write and conduct research, in particular Alessandro Valera, Julian Miglierini, Maurizio Di Franco, and Paola Barbaro.

ROME

overview centre

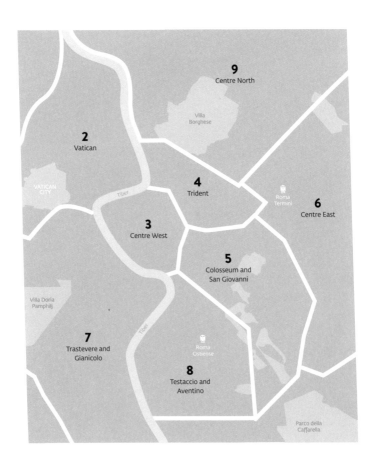

9 Centre North

Villa Borghese

2 Vatican

VATICAN CITY

Tiber

4 Trident

Roma Termini

6 Centre East

3 Centre West

5 Colosseum and San Giovanni

Villa Doria Pamphilj

Tiber

7 Trastevere and Gianicolo

Roma Ostiense

8 Testaccio and Aventino

Parco della Caffarella

ROME

overview

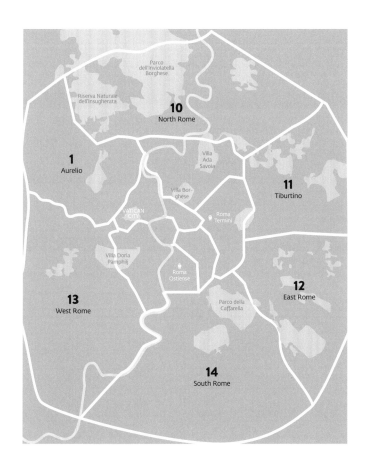

Parco
dell'Inviolatella
Borghese

Riserva Naturale
dell'Insugherata

10
North Rome

Villa
Ada
Savoia

1
Aurelio

Villa Bor-
ghese

11
Tiburtino

VATICAN
CITY

Roma
Termini

Villa Doria
Pamphilj

Roma
Ostiense

13
West Rome

Parco della
Caffarella

12
East Rome

14
South Rome

Map 1
AURELIO

Via Trionfale

Università Cattolica del Sacro Cuore

Stadio Olimpico

Foro Italico

Viale dello Stadio Olimpico

345

451

Tiber

240

Via della Pineta Sacchetti

Via di Valle Aurelia

247

Piazzale Clodio

69

Via Cipro

101

55

Via Anastasio II

447

VATICAN CITY

Map 2
VATICAN

Map 3
CENTRE WEST

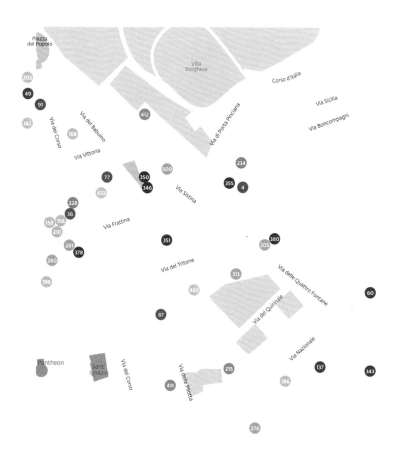

Map 4
TRIDENT

Piazza del Popolo

Villa Borghese

Corso d'Italia

202

49

91

Via Sicilia

182

Via del Babuino

412

Via di Porta Pinciana

Via Boncompagni

Via del Corso

168

Via Vittoria

500

234

77

350

346

Via Sistina

355

4

432

228

36

158

156

Via Frattina

210

351

281

306

380

378

260

Via del Tritone

313

Via delle Quattro Fontane

199

429

60

87

Via del Quirinale

Via Nazionale

Pantheon

Sant'Ignazio

Via del Corso

Via delle Piiotta

215

137

343

411

186

278

Map 5
COLOSSEUM AND
SAN GIOVANNI

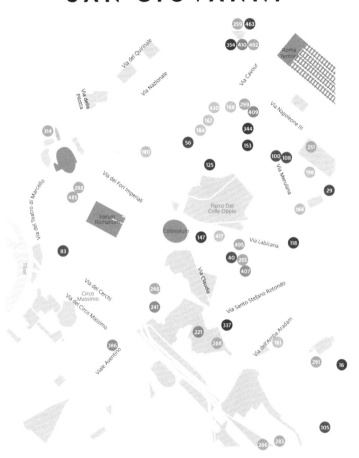

Map 6
CENTRE EAST

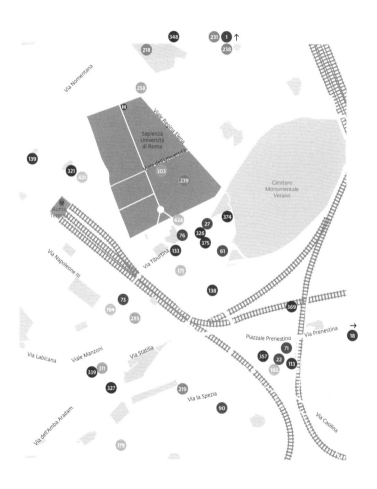

Map 7

TRASTEVERE AND
GIANICOLO

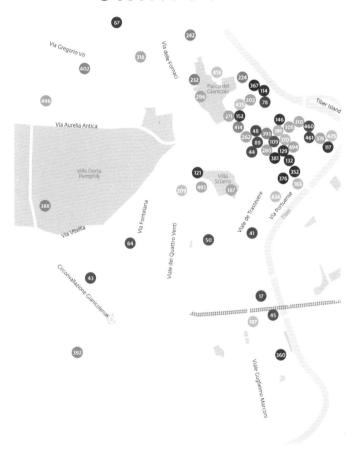

Map 8
TESTACCIO AND AVENTINO

Map 9
CENTRE NORTH

Via del Foro Italico

Via dei Campi Sportivi

Viale della Moschea

Tiber

Corso di Francia

Via Flaminia

Via Guido Reni

Via del Vignola

Villa Glori

Villa Ada Savoia

Viale Liegi

Via Salaria

Viale delle Belle Arti

Villa Borghese

Viale Giulio Cesare

Viale del Muro Torto

Corso d'Italia

Via Venti Settembre

10
98
62
8
324
122
317
453
126
85
359
35
230
264
282
385
195
395
277
243
79
185
257
483
97
353
37
401
86
329
21
178
334
307
397
92
333
94 32 180
297
415
34
452
379
141
377
95
217 23 227
74 107
46

Map 10
NORTH ROME

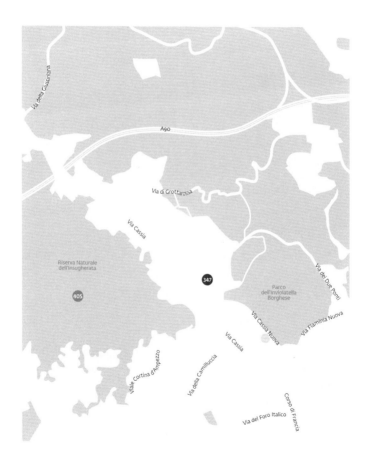

Map 11
TIBURTINO

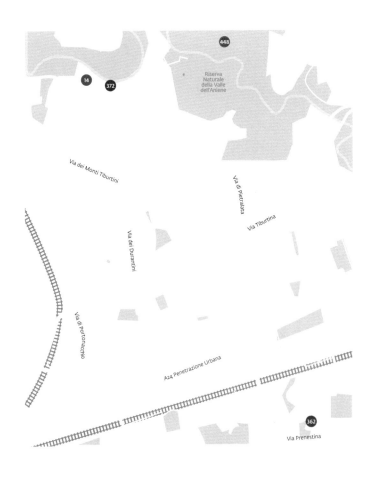

Map 12
EAST ROME

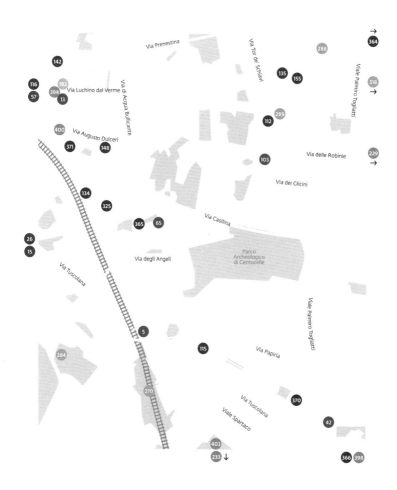

Via Prenestina

Via Tor de' Schiavi

Via di Acqua Bullicante

Via Luchino dal Verme

Via Augusto Dulceri

Via delle Robinie

Via dei Glicini

Via Casilina

Viale Palmiro Togliatti

Parco Archeologico di Centocelle

Via degli Angeli

Via Tuscolana

Viale Palmiro Togliatti

Via Papiria

Via Tuscolana

Viale Spartaco

Map 13
WEST ROME

VATICAN CITY

Via Aurelia

11

Via delle Fornaci

Via Aurelia Antica

Via Aurelia Antica

Via Leone XIII

Villa Doria Pamphilj

Viale dei Quattro Venti

Via della Nocetta

Via di Bravetta

18

Circonvallazione Gianicolense

Via del Casaletto

Viale dei Colli Portuensi

207

Via della Casetta Mattei

72

75

Via Virginia Agnelli

390

48

Via di Affogalasino

387

226

Tiber

Tiber

235 ↓

Map 14
SOUTH ROME

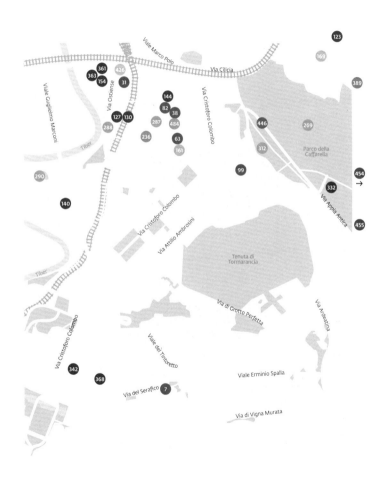

110 PLACES TO EAT OR BUY GREAT FOOD

———

5 places for a **FABULOUS BRUNCH** —————— 26

5 places for **FRESH FISH** —————————— 28

The 5 tastiest restaurants for **MEAT EATERS** ——— 30

5 of the most authentic places
for **ROMAN CUISINE** ——————————— 32

The 5 best restaurants for
INTERNATIONAL CUISINE ———————— 34

The 5 best spots for **ASIAN FOOD** ——————— 36

5 appetising places for a **VEGETARIAN MEAL** —— 38

5 cool restaurants with a **TERRACE** ——————— 41

5 must-go places for **PIZZA** ————————— 43

5 places not to miss
for **AMAZING GELATO** ———————————— 45

The 5 best places for **STREET FOOD** ——————— 47

5 places to grab a **PANINO** —————————— 49

5 favourite **OSTERIE** *to eat among the locals* ——— 51

The 5 best **GLUTEN-FREE** *options* —————— 53

5 food spots if you're **ON A BUDGET** ————— 55

5 mouth-watering places
for **CHOCOLATE LOVERS** —————————— 57

5 restaurants with
a **CONTEMPORARY TWIST** ——————————— 59

The 5 most **DELICIOUS BAKERIES** ————— 62

5 cosy **GOURMET RESTAURANTS** ————— 64

5 **PASTRY SHOPS** *not to miss* ——————— 66

5 great places to buy **GOURMET PRODUCE** —— 68

5 places to get **SPICES AND TEAS** ————— 70

5 places for a
FABULOUS BRUNCH

---

1 MOMART CAFÈ
Viale XXI Aprile 19
Centre East ⑥
+39 06 8639 1656
momartcafe.it

Modern interiors decorated with original contemporary artwork host this ample buffet-style brunch on two floors, including a large terrace. Also offers a decent *aperitivo* in the evening. Tends to get crowded, though not with tourists given its safe distance from the centre.

2 I SOFÀ
AT: HOTEL INDIGO
ROME – ST. GEORGE
Via Giulia 62
Centre West ③
+39 06 6866 1846
isofadiviagiulia.com

An oasis of modernity in one of Rome's most historic streets ensconces this American-breakfast-style brunch. Sleek interiors belie the ancient roots of this dapper hide-away. A rooftop terrace offers 360-degree views of Rome and its Renaissance rooftops.

3 MARIGOLD

**Via Giovanni
da Empoli 37
Testaccio and
Aventino** ⑧
+39 06 8772 5679
marigoldroma.com

A cafe/restaurant/bakery that brings together the best of Italian cuisine and Scandinavian design (the owners are from Copenhagen and Calabria). The menu changes weekly and features natural wine and foraged ingredients prepared in innovative ways, like stuffed bell peppers with quinoa, rice, buckwheat and tomatoes, and salsa verde. Stop by on weekends for brunch, which includes green *shakshuka,* buttermilk waffles, and sourdough pancakes.

4 HOTEL MAJESTIC ROMA

**Via Vittorio Veneto 50
Trident** ④
+39 06 421 441
hotelmajestic.com

Brunch meets La Dolce Vita at the sophisticated Hotel Majestic, situated on the renowned Via Veneto. Using organic ingredients from local farms, food ranges from beef and chicken to oysters and crepes, served on white table-cloths, surrounded by chandeliers and fresh flower arrangements.

5 GRANDMA BISTROT

**Via dei Corneli 25–27
East Rome** ⑫
+39 375 611 5695
grandmaroma.it

A hip, mid-priced *locale* off the beaten path, where the ambitious traveller is rewarded with outdoor seating, vintage furniture, tasty and modern cuisine, and an experience that makes you feel like a local. Menu options include vegetarian and vegan dishes, but the carnivore won't be disappointed.

5 places for
FRESH FISH

6 **ACQUASANTA**
Via Aldo Manuzio 28
Testaccio and
Aventino ⑧
+39 06 4555 0020
acquasantaroma.com

An industrial design with large windows and an open kitchen in the heart of Testaccio. Chef Enrico Camponeschi gets his fish directly from the daily fish auction in Anzio, a port town southwest of Rome. That old-world freshness blends well with the contemporary menu, featuring shellfish *tortello,* licorice, ginger, leeks and potatoes. Their wine list reflects that same creativity.

7 **LIVELLO 1**
Via Duccio di
Buoninsegna 25
South Rome ⑭
+39 06 503 3999
ristorantelivello1.it

Restaurant with an annexed fish shop. The menu changes daily, depending on the catch. At lunch, they offer faster and lighter options, while at dinner the dishes are creative, elegant, and all details are curated. At the bar, you can sip on a cocktail, paired with a plate of oysters.

8 **CAMPISI**
Viale Somalia 116
Centre North ⑨
+39 06 860 6634
ristorantecampisi.com

Excellent Sicilian-style fish restaurant, where most of the ingredients are brought in directly from the family business in Marzamemi (Sicily). Here the flavours of the fresh tuna fish and red prawns are glorified by pistachios, almonds, and other homemade products like orange marmalade.

9 **PIRÒ**
Vicolo della
Cancelleria 36
Centre West ③
+39 06 6880 3140
piroosteriadipesce.it

This sleek, modern restaurant is located inside a 1000-year-old building off Piazza Navona, and prides itself on serving fish caught in the surrounding Tyrrhenian sea. The place is known for its friendly staff – Chef Maurizio is said to greet every customer. The menu excels in its simplicity: lobster on a bed of *tonnarelli* pasta, yellow tomato *tortelli* in scampi *panzanella* or mollusk ravioli with crustacean sauce.

10 **MOLO 10**
Via dei Prati della
Farnesina 10
Centre North ⑨
+39 06 333 6166
molo10.it

The atmosphere is informal, with the dishes of the day written on a blackboard. Most of the fish is caught in Lazio, and is very fresh. Their forte is the plentiful starters, especially raw fish. The dishes are meticulously arranged, yet simple, with influences from fusion cuisine.

The 5 tastiest restaurants for
MEAT EATERS

---

11 FERRO E GHISA

**Circonvallazione
Aurelia 11
West Rome** ⑬
+39 06 6603 2638
ferroeghisa.com

Ferro e Ghisa specialises in grilled meats from Argentina, Denmark, the US and Italy, in a modern, lively setting. It offers a wide selection of craft beers, international wines and cocktails. Its gourmet hamburgers are decent, as are their pizzas. Be sure to book ahead, especially on the weekend.

12 CARPACCIO

**Via Ennio Quirino
Visconti 8b
Vatican** ②
+39 06 4754 8964
*carpacciothe
beefboys.com*

Dedicated to top-quality cuts of meat from around the world and Italy, this place gets its name from the Venetian painter whose works decorate this modern *locale* with sizable outdoor seating in the Prati neighbourhood. Of course, the name also refers to the thin slices of meat that they top with shaved truffle, parmigiano cheese, and other delights. But you'll also find thick, juicy slabs of Fiorentina, T-Bone, and New York Strip Steak here – even bao buns with pulled pork.

13 MR. MANZO
**Via Alberto
da Giussano 82
East Rome** ⑫
+39 06 2785 8499
ristorantepigneto.it

Pigneto is one of Rome's liveliest neighbourhoods. But Mr Manzo is on one of its quietest streets. The menu focuses on ingredients and recipes from the Marche region on the Adriatic coast, such as fresh mushrooms and truffles. The food is good and Mr Manzo is especially hospitable to large groups. Desserts are homemade.

14 BISTEAK
**Via di Pietralata 141
Tiburtino** ⑪
+39 06 4179 2126
bisteak.it

Imagine your butcher opened a restaurant inside his shop. That's the idea behind Bisteak, where customers can come to the counter and choose from a wide selection of meats, from thick Fiorentina to kebab. By the end of the night, your clothes smell like a barbecue. But you probably won't regret it.

15 I CARNIVORI
**Via Tuscolana 384
East Rome** ⑫
+39 06 7839 3058
icarnivori.com

A restaurant that prides itself on offering 'all types of meat in the world'. In truth, that translates to Chianina, Scottish, Bison, Japanese, and Argentinian. It models its decor and cooking style after the latter, which comes across as a bit gimmicky. But the quality of the meal, and the reasonable price, make up for it.

5 of the most authentic places for
ROMAN CUISINE

---

16 **SANTO PALATO**
Piazza Tarquinia 4-A/B
Colosseum and
San Giovanni ⑤
+39 06 7720 7354

This *trattoria* specialises in Rome's traditional 'fifth quarter' cuisine (i.e. offal). The rustic amuse-bouche – white pizza with mortadella (*pizza bianca e mortazza*) – is a classic, while their carbonara is considered one of the best in town. A good selection of natural wines. Daily specials posted on the wall.

17 **LA TAVERNACCIA**
Via Giovanni da
Castel Bolognese 63
Trastevere and
Gianicolo ⑦
+39 06 581 2792
latavernaccia.com

La Tavernaccia is nestled in perhaps the least touristy nook of otherwise tourist-trappy Trastevere. The pastas are meaty, cheesy, and rich, while second courses are slathered in traditional, tasty sauces. Surprisingly good service and wine.

18 **TRATTORIA
DA CESARE**
Via del Casaletto 45
West Rome ⑬
+39 06 536 015
trattoriadacesare.it

Da Cesare is a *trattoria* treasure box. Starters include perfectly fried fish, and 'gnocchi nuggets' with cheese and pepper sauce. Pastas are perfect. As for mains, Roman staples reign, such as braised oxtail, tripe with tomato and mint and fried lamb chops. The wine list is outstanding.

19 TRATTORIA PERILLI

**Via Marmorata 39
Testaccio and
Aventino** ⑧
+39 06 575 5100
perilliatestaccio.com

One of the oldest *trattorias* in Rome, dating back to 1911, spanning four generations. Its location in Testaccio, the old meatpacking district, explains its devotion to Rome's famous *quinto quarto,* or 'fifth quarter' of meat – offal. *Nervetti* (pickled cartilage), oxtail, tripe, and pork livers are mainstays, as well as other traditional Roman fare such as pasta alla carbonara, *gricia,* and *cacio e pepe.*

20 PIATTO ROMANO

**Via Giovanni
Battista Bodoni 62
Testaccio and
Aventino** ⑧
+39 06 6401 4447
piattoromano.com

A one-stop restaurant for all that Testaccio has to offer, from the neighbourhood's renowned offal dishes such as *rigatoni alla pajata, coda alla vaccinara,* and *trippa alla romana,* to some old-fashioned seasonal classics of Roman cuisine that have become hard to find, like soup with broccoli and ray.

The 5 best restaurants for
INTERNATIONAL CUISINE

---

21 BLÅ KONGO
Via Ofanto 6
Centre North ⑨
+39 06 854 6705
blakongo.com

A Swedish-international restaurant, combining ingredients and styles from Scandinavia, the Mediterranean and South Asia. The decor is minimalistic, while the menu is exciting and eclectic, including dishes like basmati rice with lemon shrimp, meatballs with jam and potatoes, and several smoked salmon combinations.

22 KALAPÀ
Via Ascoli
Piceno 17-A/B
Centre East ⑥
+39 06 8308 1997

Kalapà is a Greek restaurant famous for a speciality that's hard to find elsewhere: *kumpir e patanaki*, which are baked potatoes stuffed with a variety of fixings the customer gets to choose. The boutique interior is cosy and friendly. A nice touch: free water without having to ask, just like in Greece.

23 IPPOKRATES
Via Piave 30
Centre North ⑨
+39 06 6482 4179
ippokrates.it

Where Greeks go for Greek food. Yes, it has mandolins and Greek flags hanging on the walls. Yes, it has blue-and-white chequered table-cloths. But you'll forgive the flirtation with folky kitsch once you've tasted the delicious fava puree, eggplant with feta, and moussaka. Ouzo abounds.

24 **SAMBAMAKI**
Via Vittoria
Colonna 17
Vatican ②
+39 06 323 5178
sambamaki.com

Brazilian-Japanese fusion, the cuisine comes from Brazil's sizeable Japanese community. Dishes are small and served tapas style, letting you sample a variety of flavours, from breaded ginger chicken to teriyaki salmon and mango California rolls. It also has a sake bar and cocktail bar.

25 **MAYBU - MARGARITAS Y BURRITOS**
Via Candia 113
Vatican ②
+39 06 6941 6108
maybu.it

Maybu describes itself as high-quality Mexican fast food, although everything is made on the spot, and the ingredients are locally sourced. The menu is mercifully simple, offering tacos, burritos, salads, and nachos, all with vegetarian options, and churros for dessert. Drinks include some of the best (and only) frozen margaritas in town. In a city starved for Mexican food, Maybu's two locations are oases.

23 **IPPOKRATES**

The 5 best spots for
ASIAN FOOD

---

26 RISTORANTE MEKONG
Via Enea 56-A
East Rome ⑫
+39 06 782 5247

An excellent Vietnamese restaurant with a refined interior in the outskirts of the city. Modern paintings of the Mekong Delta add a degree of ambience without crossing into kitschville. The cuisine is on the spicy side. Try the mint-infused soups, packed with fresh veggies, rice noodles, and beef.

27 KIKO SUSHI BAR
Piazzale
del Verano 90
Centre East ⑥
+39 06 9484 9822
kikosushibar.it

Hidden behind a gas station is Kiko, which gets its name from the nickname of the restaurant's sushi sensei, Atsufumi Kikuchi, a master in his field for nearly 40 years. From the maguro rainbow rolls to the sakana tempura, the food is exquisite. It's owned by Roberto Angelini, a well-known Italian singer-songwriter.

28 DAO
Viale Jonio 328–330
North Rome ⑨
+39 06 8719 7573
daorestaurant.it

Forget the usual spring rolls, steamed rice, and almond chicken. This restaurant's creative Chinese cuisine attests to the city's growing Chinese community and its demand for variety. Mid-range prices are more than reasonable considering the excellent quality of food and decor.

29 KRISHNA 13

Via Foscolo 13
Colosseum and
San Giovanni ⑤
+39 06 700 5267
*ristoranteindia
noaroma.it*

Cosy, friendly, and busy, thanks to its reputation among locals as one of Rome's most authentic Indian restaurants. Portions are moderate, as are prices, so plan to order several dishes. Vegetarian options abound, with vegan and gluten-free dishes available.

30 SUSHISEN

Via Giuseppe
Giulietti 21-A
Testaccio and
Aventino ⑧
+39 06 575 6945
sushisen.it

A simple atmosphere in both rooms, one with Kaitenzushi or conveyor belt sushi. Ran by sake sommelier Kunihiro Este, this place was singled out by the Japanese Restaurant Organization for its quality and techniques, and its contemporary spin on traditional Japanese dishes. The vast uramaki selection matches shrimp tempura with pistachios and hazelnuts, or avocado, strawberry and red fruits.

29 KRISHNA 13

5 appetising places for a
VEGETARIAN MEAL

---

31 **ROMEOW
CAT BISTROT**
Via Francesco
Negri 15
South Rome ⑭
+39 06 5728 9203
romeowcatbistrot.com

Why watch cat videos when you can have the real deal, while sipping a hazelnut cappuccino and noshing on avocado and lime cake? True to form, these felines are largely indifferent to the customers, who come for the seasonal vegan and raw offerings. Desserts are the speciality. But savoury treats like Thai noodles and patatas bravas are also worth the visit.

32 **COL CAVOLO**
Via Cesare Bosi 7
Centre North ⑨
+39 340 863 8176

A vegan bistrot that plays on the Italian expression 'with cabbage', meaning 'nonsense'. Though there's no baloney on this menu, which puts a vegan twist on traditional Italian dishes: think lasagna made with seitan, pesto, and mushrooms. Other dishes break with tradition completely, like the peanut cream pancake with caramelised onion and apple. Save room for the vegan tiramisu and cheesecake.

34 OPS!

31 ROMEOW CAT BISTROT

33 BIBLIOTHÈ

Via Celsa 5
Centre West ③
+39 06 678 1427

Ayurvedic Indian vegetarian. For lunch, they have a 'curry in a hurry' which is a fast-track sampler of various menu items of the day on one platter. Rome is notoriously low on international food options, but Indian food is the rare exception. And Bibliothè is one that actually stands out among the Indian restaurants.

34 OPS!

Via Bergamo 56
Centre North ⑨
+39 06 841 1769
opsveg.com

If you like salad bars, this is the place for you. The buffet has a huge assortment of greens, legumes, and vegetables that you pay for by the pound. Hot dishes are prepared to order. Most ingredients are organic and many are gluten-free. A pet-friendly place with nice streetside tables.

35 BIOPOLIS CAFFÈ

Via Dire Daua 12
Centre North ⑨
+39 06 860 1315
biopolis.com

Roughly translated, 'Biopolis' means 'Organicville'. From the wine list to the herbs growing on the windowsill, this beautifully designed bar and diner lives up to its name, as does its adjacent market. Its smoothies made of seasonal fruit and veggies alone are worth the trip. It also has a nursing and baby changing area.

5 cool restaurants with a
TERRACE

36 **ZUMA RESTAURANT**
Via della Fontanella
di Borghese 48
Trident ④
+39 06 9926 6622
zumarestaurant.com

Great sushi and Japanese-fusion. The sleek interior recalls its London roots. But the rooftop terrace brings you back to Rome, with views of the Spanish Steps and the immediate surroundings, one of the city's top shopping areas. Hence the building hosting Zuma: Palazzo Fendi.

37 **CAFFÈ DELLE ARTI**
Via A. Gramsci 73
Centre North ⑨
+39 06 3265 1236
caffedelleartiroma.it

Attached to the side of the sprawling National Gallery of Modern and Contemporary Art, the cafe is an oasis of food and refreshments in an area where such is hard to come by. The surrounding open spaces make its unobstructed terrace one of the most sundrenched in town. Cuisine is classic Italian, including crisp salads. On hot days, stay inside the cool marble walls with the gorgeous statues and paintings flanking the tables.

38 LATTERIA GARBATELLA

Piazza Geremia Bonomelli 9
South Rome ⑭
+39 06 512 3913
latteriagarbatella.com

Rarely an attractive terrace is below street level. But the Garbatella neighbourhood is full of surprises, and Latteria is one of them. Ever since it opened in 2015, it has won accolades for its stellar *aperitivo,* wine and cocktails. The vintage decor and a well-stocked bar make it the perfect place to camp for the evening.

39 THE CORNER

Viale Aventino 121
Testaccio and
Aventino ⑧
+39 06 4559 7350
thecorner-roma.com/
en/restaurant

This terrace garden could be mistaken for a greenhouse, winding its way around the entire restaurant, lounge and hotel at the centre of the property. Covered tables have their own gazebo, some with stained glass. In addition to the potted herbs, plants, and flowers, there's a hanging garden.

40 LA TERRAZZA

AT: HOTEL CAPO D'AFRICA
Via Capo d'Africa 54
Colosseum and
San Giovanni ⑤
+39 06 772 801
hotelcapodafrica.com

La Terrazza has a view of the Colosseum. But what makes this terrace special is how it's nuzzled into the surrounding medieval landscape. You don't tower over the nearby churches of San Clemente and Quattro Coronati; you feel welcomed by them at eye level, surrounded by the flowers that ring the terrace edge.

5 must-go places for
PIZZA

---

41 SEU PIZZA ILLUMINATI
Via Angelo Bargoni 10
Trastevere and
Gianicolo ⑦
+39 06 588 3384
seu-pizza-illuminati.
business.site

To refer to pizza chef Daniele Seu's pies as just 'pizza' is a bit of an understatement. His menu features three sections: 'the staples', 'old school', and a longer list, 'Seu', where he gives his creativity free reign. The appetizers include Gabriele Bonci's bread with different types of extra virgin olive oil, and fried snacks.

42 SFORNO
Via Statilio Ottato
110–116
East Rome ⑫
+39 06 7154 6118
sforno.it

Italian food magazine *Agrodolce* has dubbed it the best pizza in Rome. Ironically, there's little that's Roman about it. The crust is on the thick side – crispy on the outside, but chewy on the inside. But they make up for this regional deviation with distinctly Roman toppings, such as *cacio e pepe* (pecorino and black pepper).

43 LA GATTA MANGIONA
Via F. Ozanam 30–32
Trastevere and
Gianicolo ⑦
+39 06 534 6702
lagattamangiona.com

Be sure to book ahead at Gatta Mangiona, a cat-themed *trattoria* that locals say has the best *supplì* in the city. They also do a mean *focaccia alla genovese* (with salt cod garbanzo paste) and excellent traditional pizzas. The long list of Italian and international craft beers is an added bonus.

44 PROLOCO TRASTEVERE

Via Goffredo Mameli 23
Trastevere and Gianicolo ⑦
+39 06 4559 6137
prolocotrastevere.it

A restaurant and pizzeria that doubles as a food shop specialising in cheeses and other products from the local Lazio region. Try its answer to Sunday brunch called the Peasant Lunch, consisting of various appetisers, a first or second course, and dessert. You will always find traditional Roman pasta, as well as more innovative recipes. Don't miss their craft cocktails, including the Dolspritz, made with their own signature bitter, L'Apedol.

45 SPIAZZO

Via Antonio Pacinotti 83
Trastevere and Gianicolo ⑦
+39 06 556 2738
pizzeriaspiazzo.it

Follow the ramp below street level to this hidden gem of a pizzeria, perhaps Rome's best to use an electric oven as opposed to a wood-fired one. That will lose it some points among purists, but it should earn some from those who are tired of pizza with burnt spots on the crust. Great craft beer on tap.

45 SPIAZZO

5 places not to miss for
AMAZING GELATO

---

46 COME IL LATTE
Via Silvio
Spaventa 24-26
Centre North ⑨
+39 06 4290 3882
comeillatte.it

Gelato made fresh daily. No hydrogenated fats, preservatives, artificial colours or artificial antioxidants. The main ingredient is locally sourced milk, which makes up over 60-70% of the ice cream. The rest is organic eggs and seasonal ingredients from around the world, like vanilla from Madagascar, and cinnamon from Sri Lanka.

47 GELATERIA TORCÈ
Viale Aventino 59
Testaccio and
Aventino ⑧
+39 340 522 0788
gelateriatorce.it

A pioneer of odd flavours that somehow work: gorgonzola, celery, carrot, and other ingredients that seem more appropriate at a salad bar routinely find their way into this local gelato chain. But there's plenty of traditional flavours as well, from gianduia chocolate to Sicilian pistachios. A must for gelato enthusiasts.

48 OTALEG!
Via di San
Cosimato 14-A
Trastevere and
Gianicolo ⑦
+39 338 651 5450
otaleg.com

Otaleg, or gelato spelled backwards, is a hole in the wall packed with some of the most delicious ice cream ever: thirty flavours that change with the seasons but always explode with intensity at any given time of the year (peach anyone?). Go there during the pistachio season!

49 GELATERIA DEI GRACCHI

Via di Ripetta 261
Trident ④
+39 06 322 4727
gelateriadeigracchi.it

Tucked behind Piazza del Popolo, this little spot makes for a great stop in the city centre. If you don't know which flavours to choose, go for the rich nuts, with actual chunks of dried fruit. If you're on a dairy-free diet, they have some excellent options with plant-based milk.

50 LA GOURMANDISE

Via Felice
Cavallotti 36-B
Trastevere and
Gianicolo ⑦
+39 06 9603 9081
lagourmandise.it

La Gourmandise is for purists only. There are no cones, only cups (laudably biodegradable). There's a two-flavour maximum, and some they won't let you put together because the tastes don't get along well. The owners say some recipes, such as the saffron and walnut, date back to the Renaissance.

47 GELATERIA TORCÈ

The 5 best places for
STREET FOOD

---

51 **FORNO CAMPO DE' FIORI**

Piazza Campo de' Fiori 22
Centre West ③
+39 06 6880 6662
fornocampodefiori.com

This bakery, which is tucked away in a corner of the square, behind the flower stalls, is a Roman institution, just like one of the most popular items on its shelves: the pizza bianca (or a sheet of pizza dough brushed with olive oil). Try it stuffed with mortadella (or *mortazza* in Roman), a match made in heaven.

52 **SUPPLIZIO**

Via dei Banchi Vecchi 143
Centre West ③
+39 06 8987 1920
supplizioroma.it

If you're looking for the best *supplì* in town, look no further. Arcangelo Dandini's deep-fried rice balls come with various ingredients, from tomato sauce and mozzarella cheese, to chicken gizzards, or egg and *guanciale* (pork jowl). Save some room for a chunk of fried custard cream.

53 **PANIFICIO MOSCA**

Via Candia 16
Vatican ②
+39 06 3974 2134

Panificio Mosca lures a steady stream of customers with its *maritozzo*, a little baked ball made of flour, eggs, raisins, honey, butter and salt. It's common to find them split down the middle and already filled with cream. At Panificio Mosca, they fill it with cream only once you've bought it, ensuring the freshness.

54 TRAPIZZINO

**Via Giovanni
Branca 88
Testaccio and
Aventino ⑧
+39 06 4341 9624
trapizzino.it**

In 2008, Stefano Callegari invented what would become one of Rome's most famous and popular street foods, the *trapizzino*, or a triangular pocket of pizza dough – which is crunchy on the outside and squishy inside – stuffed with classic staples of Roman cuisine, such as meatballs, or beef tongue in green sauce. Do try his chicken *cacciatore*. Some flavours are seasonal.

55 PIZZARIUM

**Via della Meloria 43
Aurelio ①
+39 06 3974 5416
bonci.it**

The place to go for any pizza lover in Rome, and absolutely worth the 10-minute walk from the Vatican. Gabriele Bonci's pizza is sold by the weight: make sure to sample different flavours as his toppings include potatoes (starch on starch is to die for), cold cuts with sun-dried tomatoes or sautéed greens with fresh mozzarella cheese.

5 places to grab a
PANINO

---

56 ZIA ROSETTA
Via Urbana 54
Colosseum and
San Giovanni ⑤
+39 06 3105 2516
ziarosetta.com

Gourmet sandwiches served on *rosetta* (rose-shaped) bread, hence the name. Ingredient options include bresaola, arugula, parmigiano cheese, strawberry balsamic reduction, bacon, smoked swordfish, guacamole, tomatoes and mint. They also offer excellent salads.

57 LA SANTERIA PIZZICHERIA – BISTROT
Via del Pigneto 213
East Rome ⑫
+39 06 6480 1606
lasanteria.it

Artisanal panini inside an impeccably designed bistro, with high-end flea-market furniture and a preponderance of antlers on the wall. There's free tap water, with a spigot sticking right out of the wall, as well as wines and desserts like New York cheesecake. Tea and coffee are served in elegant porcelain cups.

58 KNICK KNACK YODA
Piazza del
Risorgimento 11
Vatican ②
+39 06 8765 2224

The sign on the awning says Dal Papa, but don't be fooled. The only thing religious about this punk-themed joint is the devotion of its customers. The sandwiches are huge, messy, and unbelievably good. Need a burger? This is the place. Oh, and frosty IPAs are right behind you. You're welcome.

59 MORDI & VAI

AT: NUOVO MERCATO
COMUNALE DI TESTACCIO
**Via Beniamino
Franklin 12-E
Testaccio and
Aventino** ⑧
+39 339 134 3344
mordievai.it

Simple, straightforward, mouth-watering. Try Sergio Esposito's contemporary spin on sandwiches, which is always respectful of tradition. He serves Roman classics to go, between two slices of bread. If it's your first time here, start with the *allesso di scottona* (simmered beef) and chicory. He dunks the bread in the meat juices of course.

60 ER BUCHETTO

**Via del Viminale 2-F
Trident** ④
+39 329 965 2175

A Mecca for porchetta lovers, Er Buchetto (The Little Hole) lives up to its name with minimal decor and limited communal seating. But the crackly skinned, herb-rolled pork panino more than makes up for it. You may even opt to discard the bread.

60 ER BUCHETTO

5 favourite
O S T E R I E
to eat among the locals

---

61 TRAM TRAM
Via dei Reti 44–46
Centre East ⑥
+39 06 490 416
tramtram.it

Specialising in vegetable and fish classics from the southern Puglia region, this shabby-chic *locale* gets its name from the nearby tramline, which comes in handy this far from the centre. Staples are fried anchovies and fava puree with chicory.

62 LO'STERIA
Via dei Prati della
Farnesina 61
Centre North ⑨
+39 06 3321 8749
lo-steria.it

Less is more at Lo'Steria, with only a handful of items on the menu, but each perfectly executed according to Roman tradition (you'd better like your pasta carbonara al dente). Wine and beer options are plentiful in this night spot near the ancient Milvian Bridge, popular among locals, with few, if any, tourists in sight.

63 TANTO PÈ MAGNÀ
Via Giustino
de Jacobis 9–15
South Rome ⑭
+39 06 5160 7422

The aroma of down-home cooking smacks you in the face when you enter Tanto Pè Magnà. You can't go wrong with Roman classics here like *cacio e pepe* or oxtail. No matter the dish, you're bound to have plenty of juice or sauce to mop up with your bread like a pro. Italians call that tasty tactic '*scarpetta*'.

64 **OSTERIA PALMIRA**
Via Abate Ugone 29
Trastevere and
Gianicolo ⑦
+39 06 5820 4298
osteriapalmira.it

Named after Grandma Palmira. Like this restaurant's cuisine, she's from Amatrice, a beautiful hillside medieval town outside Rome famous for its guanciale, the cured pork jowl that's essential in *pasta alla gricia* and carbonara. Palmira is famous for its curled gnocchi and *ragù* made with five types of meat.

65 **OSTERIA BONELLI**
Viale dell'Acquedotto
Alessandrino 172–174
East Rome ⑫
+39 329 863 3077

It may be in the Tor Pignattara outskirts, but you'll need to book a couple days ahead at Osteria Bonelli, a favourite among locals for its stellar quality and beyond-reasonable prices. Specialities include equine dishes and superb vegetable sides.

61 TRAM TRAM

The 5 best
GLUTEN-FREE
options

---

66 **PANDALÌ**
Via di Torre
Argentina 3
Centre West ③
+39 06 6813 6731
pandali.it

Its name pays homage to Salvador Dalì, and there's a bit of that surrealist creativity at work here too. On display are the raw grains used in all their stone-ground flours: buckwheat, rice, chickpeas and corn. It's billed as a bakery, but you'll find soups and salads in addition to pizza and cake.

67 **LE ALTRE FARINE DEL MULINO**
Via di Porta
Cavalleggeri 155
Trastevere and
Gianicolo ⑦
+39 06 6440 0017

One of the best gluten-free options in the Vatican area, for breakfast, a quick lunch, and even *aperitivo* later in the day. Everything is made from scratch every day, from the croissants and the cannoli, to pizza, cookies and cakes, and tastes simply delicious.

68 EL MAÌZ - VENEZUELAN STREET FOOD

Via Tolemaide 16
Vatican ②
+39 06 6600 6878
elmaiz.it

The arepas, empanadas, and *pabellòn criollo* are highlights at Rome's only Venezuelan restaurant, that's also gluten-free. Not to be mistaken for fast food, dishes are prepared on the spot by the Moffa family, Italo-Venezuelans who migrated back to Italy in 2002. The pork, chicken, and beef stand out for their sweetness in flavour. But vegan and vegetarian options also abound.

69 PIZZERIA TERESINA SENZA GLUTINE

Via San Tommaso d'Aquino 123–125
Aurelio ①
+39 06 3903 1070
pizzeriateresina.it

This pizzeria has been famous for years as Rome's top delivery pizza. In 2015 it added gluten-free pizza to its menu, opening a separate kitchen to avoid contamination, and it's been doing extremely well since. Here you can also find gluten-free fried appetisers and lactose-free ingredients.

70 LA SOFFITTA RENOVATIO

Piazza del Risorgimento 46-A
Vatican ②
+39 06 6889 2977
lasoffittarenovatio.com

Opened in 1960 as a mom-and-pop restaurant that, thanks to its quality food and charisma, managed to attract a who's who of Italian society. Relocated to its current location in St. Peter's in 2006, La Soffita serves a menu that is largely Roman, but pays homage to the family's Abruzzo roots. It was the first pizzeria in Rome to offer Neapolitan crust, which was a sacrilege at the time, but has won it accolades as one of the best pizzerias in Rome.

5 food spots if you're
ON A BUDGET

71 DAR PARUCCA
Via Macerata 89
Centre East ⑥
+39 324 086 8361

This simple restaurant brings together sophisticated flavours and locally sourced organic ingredients. Meaty Roman treats make up the core of the menu, but you'll also find vegetarian and vegan options. Even their house wines, a Montepulciano for red and Trebbiano malvasiato for white, are organic.

72 CORNO D'AFRICA
Via Folco Portinari 7
West Rome ⑬
+39 06 5327 3923

An excellent African restaurant. Among the most popular dishes are couscous with meat and vegetables and the spiced beef stew, served with *injera*, a spongy East African sourdough flatbread. The lively restaurant only has a few tables, so be sure to book ahead.

73 RAVIOLERIA ESQUILINO
Via Principe Eugenio 80
Centre East ⑥
+39 06 9441 4767
laravioleria.it

One of Rome's coolest and tastiest take-out joints in years, combining traditional Roman fare like porchetta with Asian-fusion options like bao buns and gyoza, which makes sense in this neighbourhood known for Chinese entrepreneurs. Do yourself a favour and order a little bit of everything – or a lot of everything.

74 PINSERE

Via Flavia 98
Centre North ⑨
+39 06 4202 0924

This *locale* specialises in *pinsa*, an oval-shaped focaccia bread that dates back to ancient Rome, but today is a rarity. Toppings are manifold: ham and figs, parmigiana, cacio e pepe, pumpkin flowers, ricotta, lard, sardines, and mozzarella are just a few. Pinsere also offers cold pastas and salads.

75 FINGER

Piazza Pietro
Merolli 53
West Rome ⑬
+39 06 8379 6538

High-quality fast food. There's only seating for 15 at Finger plus some standing and leaning room at the counter. Dishes include cedar-infused artichokes and saffron-battered vegetables. Food changes daily, depending on what's fresh at the market. But you can always count on cold craft brews and good wine.

5 mouth-watering places for
CHOCOLATE LOVERS

76 **SAID DAL 1923**
Via Tiburtina 135
Centre East ⑥
+39 06 446 9204
said.it

Rome doesn't automatically come to mind when thinking of the world's best chocolate. But Said is one of Italy's many stellar chocolateries vying to change that. Tucked down a small courtyard, this deceptively cavernous-yet-cosy chocolate factory makes some of the thickest hot chocolate around.

77 **QUETZALCOATL CHOCOLATIER**
Via delle Carrozze 26
Trident ④
+39 06 6920 2191
chocolatissimo.it

Not a shop to duck in and out of. The shopkeepers want to tell you about their gourmet chocolate while you indulge. They also have delicious ice cream with exotic flavours, such as the tonka bean, which is illegal in some countries. What you buy is wrapped in a box so pretty you'll want to keep it.

78 **RIVENDITA LIBRI CIOCCOLATA E VINO**
Vicolo del Cinque 11-A
Trastevere and Gianicolo ⑦
+39 06 5830 1868

Books, chocolate, and wine. What more could you ask for? The speciality of the house is a little cup made of chocolate filled with liquor and topped with cream. The bohemian store is eclectically decorated with a piano, a preponderance of chandeliers and drapery.

79 GAY ODIN

Via Antonio
Stoppani 9
Centre North ⑨
+39 06 8069 3023
gay-odin.it

Slow-roasted, at low heat in a wood-burning oven. That's the secret behind the cacao beans at Gay Odin. It's been in Naples for more than 100 years and in Rome since 2001. We particularly like the nut flavours, from Pugliese almonds to Sorrento walnuts and Giffoni hazelnuts.

80 CONFETTERIA MORIONDO E GARIGLIO

Via del Piè di
Marmo 21–22
Centre West ③
+39 06 699 0856
moriondoegariglio.com

Originally from Turin, this old-style chocolate shop continues to produce artisan chocolate, according to tradition and family recipes. Pralines come both in milk and dark chocolate and the fillings include classic flavours as well as more experimental ones. If you're looking for a gift, then ask them to fill a beautiful red box with your own selection.

76 SAID DAL 1923

5 restaurants with a
CONTEMPORARY TWIST

81 **RETROBOTTEGA**
Via della Stelletta 4
Centre West ③
+39 06 6813 6310
retro-bottega.com

Simple, quick and refined – three things that rarely go together in the historic centre of Rome. The open kitchen is staffed by young cooks trained in Michelin-starred restaurants. Service is minimal, with a 'grab your own drink from the fridge' policy. The menu changes often, but dishes always feature wild herbs, roots, tubers, flowers, and fruits, which they forage themselves.

82 **BAUHAUS ROME**
Piazza Eugenio Biffi 3
South Rome ⑭
+39 06 8538 8481

Rome's residential Garbatella neighbourhood might be the last place you'd expect this modern gem. Built inside a historic bakery, the ground floor still produces its own sourdough bread and pizzas, with the dining room upstairs, offering American breakfasts, business lunches, and scrumptious tasting menus including amberjack and apricot sashimi, fried anchovies with blueberry vinaigrette salad, and *spaghettone* with raw pink prawns.

81 RETROBOTTEGA

84 PER ME – GIULIO TERRINONI

83 RHINOCEROS ENTR'ACTE

Via dei Cerchi 19-23
Colosseum and
San Giovanni ⑤
+39 360 103 4177
rhinocerosentracte.com

A contemporary art space with a restaurant and terrace overlooking ancient Roman ruins. Designed by architect Jean Nouvel, this space hosts exhibitions, multimedia installations, events and performances. Both decor and menu are inspired by the African savanna. In order to eat, you're required to visit the gallery as well.

84 PER ME – GIULIO TERRINONI

Vicolo del Malpasso 9
Centre West ③
+39 06 687 7365
giulioterrinoni.it

This Michelin-starred restaurant is intimate, as are its minimalist dishes – *i tappi* – that come in tapas-size, so order several. The prices are surprisingly reasonable, but that applies only to lunch-time. The chef, Giulio Terrinoni, literally wrote the book on sea urchins, and concentrates on sustainable seafood, so you won't find tuna. The fish is excellent. But so is the meat. And everything else.

85 BISTROT64

Via Guglielmo
Calderini 64
Centre North ⑨
+39 06 323 5531
bistrot64.it

Possibly the most affordable Michelin-starred restaurant in Italy: they charge just 60 euro for a great five-course meal, with a selection of dishes chosen by the Japanese chef Noda Kotaro. He combines excellent technique, locally-sourced high-quality ingredients, and Italian and Japanese traditions. This contemporary bistro proves that extraordinary food doesn't have to break the bank.

The 5 most
DELICIOUS BAKERIES

---

86 **SANTI SEBASTIANO E VALENTINO**
Via Tirso 107
Centre North ⑨
+39 06 8756 8048

This old-timey bakery (opened in 2015) only uses unprocessed flours and old-fashioned Italian and German recipes. Apart from scrumptious breads and desserts, they also serve carb-based dinners, such as pizza, lasagna and cannelloni, served on very nice marble tabletops.

87 **L'ANTICO FORNO**
Via delle Muratte 8
Trident ④
+39 06 679 2866

A jewel in a tourist cesspool. Indeed, the front end is guilty of selling souvenirs. But squeeze your way to the back bakery, and treasures await: some of the best, most reasonably priced pizza, bread, and other baked goods in the whole city.

88 **PANIFICIO PASSI**
Via di Mastro Giorgio 87
Testaccio and Aventino ⑧
+39 06 574 6563

Brace yourself for the sharp elbows of the loyal grannies who shop at Panificio Passi, a bakery frozen in the 1970s, as are some of its prices: pizza rossa goes for 12,50 euro per kilo. It also sells cured meat, pizza, and pre-cooked dishes. The house speciality is *pane azzimo*, a crunchy bread made without yeast.

89 LE LEVAIN

Via Luigi Santini 22
Trastevere and
Gianicolo ⑦
+39 06 6456 2880
lelevainroma.it

Bread and pastry lovers may sometimes find Roman creations over-sweetened and under-buttered. Le Levain is the antidote, a perfect fusion of French and Italian, where the croissants are savoury and the cheesecake is creamy. The wide selection of snack-sized paninos on fresh-made bread match well with an impressive selection of French and Italian wine and beer.

90 GASTROMARIO

Via Voghera 10
Centre East ⑥
+39 06 7978 2584

A French-inspired bakery and pastry shop that's also a restaurant-cafe, serving biodynamic wines and microbrews. Its leafy patio makes it a great place to escape the sun on a hot day. It easily boasts the best bread on this side of the Eternal City, plus a novel decor and charming staff.

89 LE LEVAIN

5 cosy
GOURMET
RESTAURANTS

---

91 **ACQUOLINA RISTORANTE**
AT: THE FIRST ROMA
Via del Vantaggio 14
Trident ④
+39 06 320 1590
acquolinaristorante.it

This Michelin-starred restaurant is a great spot if you find yourself in the Piazza del Popolo neighbourhood. The artistic, fish-centric cuisine comes in both dinner-size and tasting portions. Situated within The First Roma Arte hotel, you can choose between a ground floor restaurant or the panoramic view on the roof.

92 **ALL'ORO, THE H'ALL TAILOR SUITE**
Via Giuseppe Pisanelli 23–25
Centre North ⑨
+39 06 9799 6907
ristorantealloro.it

A decadent hotel restaurant that's won every medal in the book for its refined cuisine, with both classic Italian and avant-garde influences. Consider the 'tiramisù' of potatoes, salt cod and cinta senese bacon, or the the superb Roman-style lamb, if on the menu. One Michelin star.

93 **CASA BLEVE**
Via del Teatro Valle 48
Centre West ③
+39 06 686 5970
casableve.com

An upscale wine bistro in the courtyard of a 15th-century palazzo, with an impressive list of mostly cold appetisers like beef and fish tartare, or pumpkin flower stuffed with ricotta and pistachio. They also have exquisite warm dishes. The wine list, like the ancient underground cellar, is impressive.

94 MARZAPANE

Via Velletri 39
Centre North ⑨
+39 06 6478 1692
marzapaneroma.com

Different types of menus for different occasions and palates, including a special three-course lunch menu on Mondays, Thursdays, and Fridays. Particularly intriguing is the chef's table, as the menu is meant to be shared, and covers several cooking techniques, like smoking, grilling, *flambadou,* or using ash and clay.

95 RISTORANTE CHINAPPI

Via Augusto
Valenziani 19
Centre North ⑨
+39 06 481 9005
chinappi.it

A tried and true gourmet fish restaurant, with a reputation for the freshest catch in the city, and the best octopus you've ever tasted - first boiled, then grilled. You can choose among several different menus, starting from 50 euro per person (drinks not included). The atmosphere is quite elegant and welcoming.

5
PASTRY SHOPS
not to miss

---

96 **CASA MANFREDI**
Viale Aventino 91-93
Testaccio and
Aventino ⑧
+39 06 9760 5892
casamanfredi.it

Known as one of Rome's best pastry shops, Casa Manfredi also churns out artisanal gelato made with exquisite ingredients such as Domori chocolate, Alphonso mangoes, and Feudo San Biagio pistachios. Also specialises in cakes you can customise yourself using the Casa Manfredi app.

97 **PASTICCERIA GRUÉ**
Viale Regina
Margherita 95-99
Centre North ⑨
+39 06 841 2220
gruepasticceria.it

Stylish patisserie and cafe specialising in craft chocolates, gelato, *panettone* and macarons. Known for the kind service and clean interior, Grué is close to the eclectically baroque neighbourhood of Coppedè, and is a good pitstop on the way to Villa Borghese.

98 **MONDI**
Via Flaminia 468
Centre North ⑨
+39 06 333 6466
pasticceriamondi.com

No frills for this historic pastry shop, just a few steps away from one of the most popular nightlife areas. For generations it has delighted locals with sweets, gelato, pastries, and pralines. It's also a great spot to grab a panino for lunch, or a good cocktail in the evening.

99 PASTICCERIA WALTER MUSCO

Largo Benedetto
Bompiani 8–10
South Rome ⑭
+39 06 512 4103
*pasticceria
waltermusco.it*

Walter Musco's pastries are conceptual
and extraordinarily delicious at once. He
applies the motto 'Less is more' to desserts.
A self-taught pastry chef, he mixes technical
mastery with prime quality ingredients, and
a solid aesthetic philosophy that constantly
reinvents the tradition. Can a Brancusi
sculpture or a Jackson Pollock painting
be turned into a chocolate Easter egg?
Come and see for yourself.

100 PASTICCERIA REGOLI

Via dello Statuto 60
Colosseum and
San Giovanni ⑤
+39 06 487 2812
pasticceriaregoli.com

An artisan pastry shop founded in 1916.
Located a stone's throw from Santa Maria
Maggiore and Piazza Vittorio Emanuele II,
this historic bakery carefully selects
its raw materials, which shine through
in their almond tart with apricot and
sour cherry jam, but especially in the
traditional *maritozzi con la panna,* among
the best in town.

96 CASA MANFREDI

5 great places to buy
GOURMET PRODUCE

101 LA TRADIZIONE
Via Cipro 8
Aurelio ①
+39 06 3972 0349
latradizione.it

An extraordinary deli not far from the Vatican museums. In this gourmet shop you'll find prime quality cheese and cured meats. The produce is not just Roman, as they carry rare food from all over the world. They also have fresh pasta, pickled vegetables, wines, oils, truffles and refined takeaway dishes like fish salad.

102 ERCOLI 1928
Via Montello 26
Vatican ②
+39 06 372 0243
ercoli1928.com

A historic gourmet shop, featured in Giacomo Balla's 1942 *The Queue for Lamb* (at GNAM in Rome), it's evolved also into a restaurant and bar at a second location in Parioli. Besides cheese and cured meats, you'll find balsamic vinegar, olive oil, mustards, smoked wild salmon, caviar and other delicacies from abroad.

103 PROLOCO – DOL
Via Domenico
Panaroli 35
East Rome ⑫
+39 06 2430 0765
dioriginelaziale.it

There's perhaps no better place in the capital to try quality local produce, meats, and cheeses. Products are sourced exclusively from local artisans in the Lazio region by a team of young entrepreneurs. The cured meats like *corallina romana* and *mangalitza* boar are especially good.

104 SALUMERIA VOLPETTI

Via Marmorata 47
Testaccio and
Aventino ⑧
+39 375 513 0898
volpetti.com

Another historic location for gourmets in Rome. This high-end deli, which opened in 1973, sells Italian and international cold cuts (from prosciutto crudo to pata negra) and cheese (mountain, goat, Parmigiano), olive oil and preserved vegetables. Around the corner, at Via Alessandro Volta 8, you'll find the Taverna, where you can sit and enjoy a meal with products from the shop, including wines.

105 LA FORMAGGERIA

Mercato Piazza
Epiro, Box 25–26
Colosseum and
San Giovanni ⑤
+39 328 466 8373
laformaggeriaroma.it

No need for a map – you can smell your way to this cheese stand at the Mercato Latino. The selection is truly remarkable in quality and quantity: about 140 different types, mostly from small producers, with an emphasis on blue cheeses, and only a few yet targeted varieties from outside Italy.

5 *places to get*
SPICES AND TEAS

---

106 **BIBLIOTÈQ TEA SHOP**
Via dei Banchi
Vecchi 124
Centre West ③
+39 06 4543 3114
biblioteq.it

This shop offers an incredible array of items, including flavoured tea-based mixtures. The loose teas – over 150 varieties kept in their red, black, and green containers – come from China, Japan, India, Ceylon, Nepal, Vietnam, and Africa.

107 **IL GENOVINO D'ORO**
Via Collina 22
Centre North ⑨
+39 339 527 0975
italyexport.com

The owner, Franco Calafatti, personally mixes together and grinds salt, leaves, roots, and berries from Italy and abroad. His love and passion for the subject matter is contagious. The shop often organises culinary events and classes on how to integrate spices in your recipes.

108 **SELLI INTERNATIONAL FOOD STORE**
Via dello
Statuto 28–30
Colosseum and
San Giovanni ⑤
+39 06 474 5777

In the heart of an ethnically cosmopolitan neighbourhood, this shop carries spices and cereals from all over the world, together with international drinks, and packaged foods such as sauces, canned coconut milk and snacks. The products are fresh and can be bought by weight.

109 DROGHERIA INNOCENZI
**Via Natale
del Grande 31
Trastevere and
Gianicolo** ⑦
+39 06 581 2725

Step inside this old-style grocer's, and you'll be welcomed with extreme courtesy. All three rooms in the store are filled to the ceiling with bags of teas and spices from India, China, and Japan, coffees and chocolate from Italy, legumes, rice, candies, exotic sauces and dried fruits from several countries in the world.

110 EMPORIO DELLE SPEZIE
**Via Galvani 11
Testaccio and
Aventino** ⑧
+39 327 861 2655
emporiodellespezie.com

Let the sweet and pungent smell of the spices and teas envelop you as you enter this tiny microcosm of flavours, where you can buy herbs and powders by weight. Their pepper selection is quite impressive. You'll also find recipes and inspiration for using these aromas in new inviting combinations.

106 BIBLIOTÈQ TEA SHOP

THE JERRY THOMAS PROJECT

45 PLACES FOR A DRINK

---

5 of the best places for **CRAFT BEER** —————— 74

5 of the coolest speakeasies for
proper **COCKTAILS** —————— 76

5 places with an excellent **WINE LIST** —————— 78

5 funky **DISCOS AND CLUBS** —————— 80

5 great places to **DRINK ON A BUDGET** ———— 82

5 places for **SMOKERS** —————— 84

5 **GOURMET COFFEE** bars —————— 86

5 **GAY-FRIENDLY BARS AND CLUBS** ——— 88

5 charming places to sip on an **APERITIVO** ——— 90

5 of the best places for
CRAFT BEER

---

111 HOPSIDE
Via Francesco
Negri 39
Testaccio and
Aventino ⑧
+39 06 6931 3081
hopside.it

Terrific craft beer brewed on site, plus a big selection of brews on tap from elsewhere in Italy, which the staff is constantly rotating. The food is a delicious mix of Italian and international food, i.e. good pastas and burgers, plus a lot of options for vegetarians and the health-conscious, like quinoa and soy.

112 MAD HOP
Via Tor de' Schiavi 231
East Rome ⑫
+39 06 3107 6166

A very friendly brewery, with the kind of young and fun managers that typify the Centocelle neighbourhood, and make it worth the trek. In addition to their wide selection of local beers, they also boast a healthy selection of amaros and digestivos from right here in the province of Rome.

113 BIRRA+
Via del Pigneto 105
Centre East ⑥
+39 06 7061 3106
birrapiu.it

The 'Beer' part refers to the six quality Italian brews they always have on tap, changing the selection daily. The 'Plus' part refers to the deep Scotch list: Bunnahabhain, Glenfarclas, Bruichladdich, and Ardbeg are just a few. They offer a true happy hour with 4-euro pours Sunday to Thursday, from 5 to 8 pm.

114 MA CHE SIETE VENUTI A FÀ

**Via Benedetta 25
Trastevere and
Gianicolo ⑦
+39 06 6456 2046**
football-pub.com

This pub changed the way Romans perceive beer, by promoting craft beers from micro-breweries. They have 16 beers on tap, including some of the best national and international brands. It's tiny and in the very heart of Trastevere, so always packed with people. Also very popular during football matches.

115 BARLEY WINE

**Viale dei
Consoli 115–117
East Rome ⑫
+39 06 4568 7489**
barleywine.it

Nine Italian craft beers on tap, plus bottled beers all made with spontaneous fermentation. The ambience is decidedly chill, with comfy couches and classic tables, inside and out. Their organic sourdough focaccias are made by the same people behind Grandma Bistrot.

111 HOPSIDE

5 of the coolest speakeasies for proper COCKTAILS

116 **SPIRITO**
   Via Fanfulla
   da Lodi 53
   East Rome ⑫
   +39 327 298 3900
   club-spirito.com

Spirito is fronted by a small sandwich shop with a payphone on the back wall. Payphone? Who uses a payph...Aha! You enter by ringing the gatekeeper, who sneaks you through a refrigerator door into the back room ten times bigger, with a sexy rooftop terrace.

117 **MARIA SABINA WILD SPIRITS**
   Via di Santa Cecilia 8
   Trastevere and
   Gianicolo ⑦
   +39 348 587 1914

This speakeasy is located in the crypt beneath La Punta Mexican restaurant. Expect an Ayahuasca-inspired experience, with mezcal and tequila-based cocktails that are named after the five senses. It gets its name from the legendary *curandera* María Sabina Magdalena García, who helped introduce psychedelic mushrooms to Westerners in the early 20th century.

118 **THE BARBER SHOP**
   Via Iside 6
   Colosseum and
   San Giovanni ⑤
   +39 389 508 6037
   thebarbershoproma.it

You guessed it – this speakeasy near the Colosseum is fronted by a barbershop. Once the sun sets, it opens its cellar doors to a hidden piano lounge with Persian rugs, cold cocktails and a warm energy, that commonly stays open until sunrise. Paid membership required.

119 THE JERRY THOMAS PROJECT

Vicolo Cellini 30
Centre West ③
+39 06 9684 5937
thejerrythomasproject.it

A pioneer of the Rome speakeasy scene, The Jerry Thomas Project takes some homework. First you need to call ahead for the password, which they'll e-mail you, or check the clues on the website. Then you have to pay a modest membership fee. Doors are open from 10 pm until the wee hours. Smoking is permitted.

120 ARGOT

Via dei Cappellari 93
Centre West ③
+39 06 4555 1966
argotmixology.
business.site

There's no sign on this speakeasy behind Campo de' Fiori, so instead, look for the well-dressed bouncer near the crossroads with Via di Montoro. Two rooms: one with a piano lounge, another a smoker's lounge. There's often live music, tending towards jazz, blues, and soul. Membership fee required.

119 THE JERRY THOMAS PROJECT

5 *places with an excellent*
WINE LIST

---

121 **LA MESCITA MONTEVERDE**
Via Fratelli Bonnet 5
Trastevere and
Gianicolo ⑦
+39 349 613 4850

Same place as the defunct Litro, similar concept, but different people behind this new bistro in the residential Monteverde neighbourhood, specialising in natural wines, i.e. made without adding or removing anything during winemaking, paired with cold dishes. Vintages are changed weekly.

122 **MOSTÒ**
Viale Pinturicchio 32
Centre North ⑨
+39 392 257 9616

Mostò strikes a friendly note with its large community table, and only a few small tables off to the sides, making it easy to meet fellow imbibers. The wine list puts an emphasis on natural wines, local vintages, as well as French. Food options include sandwiches, cured meats and cheeses, and warm snacks like meatballs and eggplant rolls.

123 VINUM EST

Via Francesco Valesio 24
South Rome ⑭
+39 06 785 3806
vinumest.it

A spacious *enoteca*/speciality food store off the Alberone street market, offering myriad bottles of wines and spirits, all strictly organised by their Italian region of provenance. The counter is well stocked with meats, cheeses, and other delicacies that the passionate owner will gladly tell you about as you sample his goods.

124 BANCOVINO

Via Pietro Borsieri 27
Vatican ②
+39 06 855 1592
bancovino.com

By day, Bancovino is a gourmet food market. By night, it's a winery. Located in the upscale Prati neighbourhood, it takes its name from the steel community counter that runs through the middle of the shop, providing both seating and prep space for all the food.

125 VINOROMA

Via in Selci 84-G
Colosseum and San Giovanni ⑤
+39 347 892 6336
vinoroma.com

A natural wine oasis in Rome's hip Monti neighbourhood, just minutes from the Colosseum. Owner and sommelier Maurizio Di Franco (Italian-American) calls on his vast network of producers to host vineyard-to-table tastings of some of the most interesting wines in Italy. You'll be blown away by their medieval wine cellar. They also organise walking food and drink tours around the city.

5 funky
DISCOS AND CLUBS

126 **FORTE ANTENNE**
**Via del Forte
Antenne 12
Centre North** ⑨
+39 333 865 4933

An underground fort dating back to 1877, completely made of tuffa and bricks. There's even a dry moat. The site is located where the ancient city of Antemnae once stood. Abandoned for decades, the fort was turned into a social club in 2021, which now hosts dinners, DJ sets, concerts, and other events.

127 **CIRCOLO DEGLI ILLUMINATI**
**Via Giuseppe
Libetta 1
South Rome** ⑭
+39 327 761 5286
circolodegliilluminati.it

This venue quickly established itself as one of the main underground clubs in town. From Thursday to Saturday, until 5 am, it hosts international DJs and live sets, with electronic, techno, and house music. Saturday is the best night, with the Minù Party. Three rooms plus a garden. Let your freak flag fly.

128 LARGO VENUE

Via Biordo
Michelotti 2
Centre East ⑥
+39 06 5987 5966
largovenue.com

Largo epitomises the bohemian Pigneto neighbourhood. Much like the rest of the area, it was built out of industrial ruins, with a sprawling interior and outdoor garden that often doubles as an art space during the day. But the night belongs to music, ranging from industrial and experimental to electronic rock and DJ sets. If you're wondering where Rome's edgy avant-garde crowd hangs out, this is it.

129 ALCAZAR LIVE

Via Cardinale
Merry del Val 14-B
Trastevere and
Gianicolo ⑦
+39 339 127 8354
alcazarlive.it

Live music, theatrical performances, art installations, and art-house film screenings are the bread and butter of Alcazar Live, a retro movie theatre turned mixed-use space. It also boasts a full-service restaurant and Sunday brunch. Alcazar Live also organises free live music and outdoor performances on the terrace of Gianicolo Hill.

130 RASHŌMON CLUB

Via degli
Argonauti 16
South Rome ⑭
+39 391 730 7386
rashomonclub.com

One of the biggest dance clubs this close to the centre of Rome, where true clubbers feel at home. It offers two rooms, a cocktail bar, and an outdoor garden setup in the Garbatella neighbourhood. Rashōmon primarily hosts house and techno DJs. While the music is loud, the vibe is very laidback and casual, unlike a lot of Roman clubs where you're expected to dress up.

5 great places to
DRINK ON A BUDGET

131 **IL VINAIETTO**
  Via del Monte
  della Farina 38
  Centre West ③
  +39 06 6880 6989

This loveable vineria should be on everyone's list, not just wine-lovers, but lovers of local colour. The clientele is a broad spectrum of Roman society, and the mood is always cheery. Afterall, with generous pours of quality wine at roughly 5 euro per glass, why wouldn't it be?

132 **LETTERE CAFFÈ**
  Via San Francesco
  a Ripa 100–101
  Trastevere and
  Gianicolo ⑦
  +39 340 004 4154

One of the few *locali* in Trastevere to retain its bohemian aura, Lettere Caffè lives up to its name, offering a selection of subversive and anarchist literature in a small reading nook at the entrance, as well as beer, wine and cocktails throughout. There's also live music. Joan Baez would feel at home.

133 **BAR DEI BRUTTI**
  Via dei Volsci 71–73
  Centre East ⑥
  +39 06 8901 3825

The ironic name – Bar of the Uglies – should say something about the sense of humour that permeates this college hangout. It's also the kind of bar where you can spend hours and hours, reading a book or using the free Wi-Fi, even after you have finished your coffee, without getting the evil eye.

134 SHAKESPEARE & CO.

Via dei Savorgnan 72
East Rome ⑫
+39 333 360 0506

Tucked away in the timeless Certosa neighbourhood lies Shakespeare & Co., an *enoteca*-cum-bookstore. The owner is a sommelier with a passion for small publishing houses. In the back there's a garden named Patio Marquez, after the writer who died the day this shop opened. A real treat.

135 L'OMBRALONGA

Via Federico
Delpino 110
East Rome ⑫
+39 377 089 3293

This bar gets its name from a term in the Veneto region that means to drink several glasses. Indeed, the owners are from the Veneto region, and like all good Venetians, know how to mix a good Spritz, both with Aperol or Campari. The average price is 3 euro, which is refreshingly more Venetian than Roman as well.

131 IL VINAIETTO

5 places for
SMOKERS

---

136 FINCATO – LA CASA DEL HABANO
Via della Colonna Antonina 34
Centre West ③
+39 06 678 5508
fincatolacasa delhabano.com

Many an Italian politician has been spied smoking a fat Cuban stogie outside Fincato, located a stone's throw from both the prime minister's office (Palazzo Chigi) and the Italian Chamber of Deputies (Palazzo Montecitorio). The modest façade disguises its voluminous offerings of fine tobacco, with a very knowledgeable staff.

137 SA TANCA CROSTACERIA
Via Palermo 57
Trident ④
+39 328 907 0650
satancacrostaceria.com

Winston Churchill would feel at home in Sa Tanca Crostaceria, a seafood restaurant, oyster bar, and cigar room. Crystal chandeliers, gold-painted furniture and red-velvet upholstery exude a high-roller ambience, but without going overboard. The liquor list runs deep, and the wine cellar is worth a visit.

138 CANAPA CAFFÈ

Viale dello Scalo
San Lorenzo 30
Centre East ⑥
+39 351 035 2704
canapacaffe.net

Rome will never be Amsterdam. But at least you can find cappuccino made with hemp milk at this bar, which also serves a variety of cannabis-based foods, albeit without THC, the active agent in marijuana. If you have a medicinal marijuana prescription, you can partake in the real thing inside the Therapy Room.

139 BABBO'S

Via Volturno 13
Centre East ⑥
+39 06 474 1322
babbos.it

A restaurant specialising in steak and fish, with a smoking section. The owners pride themselves on creative-yet-traditional Tuscan cuisine, with homemade pastas and desserts. Vegetarian and gluten-free options available. Also serves Naples-style pizza.

140 TABACCHERIA VANNICELLI DAL 1954

Viale Guglielmo
Marconi 600
South Rome ⑭
+39 06 557 6205
*tabaccheria
vannicelli.it*

A family-run tobacco shop worth its smoke, specialising in Cuban and Italian cigars and pipes from around the world, and boasting a walk-in humidor. A corner of the store is devoted to books and research materials on the merchandise. The shop hosts literature and music events in the evening, and several cigar clubs.

5
GOURMET COFFEE
bars

---

141 FARO – LUMINARI DEL CAFFÈ
Via Piave 55
Centre North ⑨
+39 06 4281 5714
farorome.com

Speciality coffee is the star of the menu at this Northern-European looking bar, be it an espresso or a French press coffee. The go-to beans are from Ruben Gardelli, but the weekly selection rotates. And you can also buy the gear for home-brewing here.

142 FAX FACTORY
Via Antonio
Raimondi 87
East Rome ⑫
+39 06 6930 1043
faxfactory.it

Half art gallery, showcasing works from local artists, and half speciality coffee Mecca, with beans both from Italy and from international roasters and several different brewing methods available. The seating is limited, but the vibes are cool and relaxed.

143 ROSCIOLI CAFFÈ PASTICCERIA
Piazza Benedetto
Cairoli 16
Centre West ③
+39 06 8916 5330
rosciolicaffe.com

It's not always easy to find great coffee in tourist areas. But Roscioli is the exception to the rule. The espresso machine has been modified to include different coffee-making methods. There are only five other ones like it in the world. They always use arabica beans, from Latin America, India and Africa, depending on the season.

144 NERO VANIGLIA

**Circonvallazione
Ostiense 201
South Rome** ⑭
+39 06 578 0306

This pastry shop is quickly establishing itself as a reference point for the neighbourhood, as it fits in the spaces of the historic Gori laboratory. Besides delicious pastries, they serve excellent coffee, from Oro Caffè for the espresso, and Ditta Artigianale and Edo Quarta speciality coffee, for the v60, french press and cold brew.

145 PERGAMINO CAFFÈ

**Piazza del
Risorgimento 7
Vatican** ②
+39 06 8953 3745

Pergamino is emphatic about not being a bar. It's a coffee shop. A moot distinction in most Roman cafes, but not here, where coffee takes centre stage. It's always freshly ground on the spot, from classic Italian espresso to filtered or infused. Pergamino also offers dynamite pastries, such as tiramisu, muffins and cheesecake.

141 FARO – LUMINARI DEL CAFFÈ

5

GAY-FRIENDLY BARS AND CLUBS

---

146 LIBRERIA TUBA

**Via del Pigneto 39-A
Centre East** ⑥
+39 06 7039 9437
libreriatuba.it

A funky cafe/bookstore opened and run by a group of feminists in the heart of Pigneto's hip 'pedestrian island', with one of the best patios in the neighbourhood. By night, it combines cocktails with roundtables on feminist literature (the name 'Tuba' means fallopian tube in Italian). By day, it serves great cappuccino and croissants.

147 MY BAR

**Via di San Giovanni
in Laterano 12
Colosseum and
San Giovanni** ⑤
+39 06 700 4425

Close to the Colosseum, it's only natural that My Bar would get its fair share of tourists by day. But by night, the vibe takes on a rainbow hue, with the pride flag hoisted high at the entrance. The enviable street terrace makes it a communal space for all walks of life. It's also a good spot for karaoke.

148 K MEN CLUB

Via Amati Amato 6–8
East Rome ⑫
+39 349 587 6731
kmenclub.com

A techno-infused gay sex club with a variety of constantly changing themes, from rubber and leather to nude nights. There are both private rooms and public spaces, glory holes and mazes. Check the website for the dress code (or non-dress code) on the night you want to visit.

149 POPPE PARTY

VARIOUS LOCATIONS

The dance party that celebrates Britney Spears, Backstreet Boys, Mariah Carey, Spice Girls, and all the best – but mostly the worst – pop music ever. So if you're not that innocent, and you want it that way, head to POPPE Party to live your sweet, sweet fantasy and spice up your life. Check their Facebook page for dates and locations.

150 MUCCASSASSINA

AT: QUBE DISCO
Via di
Portonaccio 212
Tiburtino ⑪
muccassassina.com

Muccassassina (The Killer Cow) is Rome's most legendary gay club, open only on Fridays. It started in the early 90s as a fundraiser for gay rights initiatives. Since then it has become something of an institution in Italy thanks to the quality of its music and the celebrities who come here to party. The music is loud. The beats are fast. The DJs (often) wear nothing but thongs.

5 charming places to sip on an
APERITIVO

---

151 CHORUS CAFÉ
**Via della
Conciliazione 4
Vatican ②
+39 06 6889 2774**
choruscafe.it

This elegant cocktail bar and restaurant, in the mezzanine of the Auditorium della Conciliazione, with muted lighting and a pared down look, serves refined drinks, created by the expert mixologist Massimo D'Addezio. The list of signature cocktails includes the Chorus Sauar (sic), Bloody Max, 17 e Mezzo and Japanese 75. All alcoholic beverages cost 18 euro. For the over-35 crowd.

152 IL BARETTO
**Via Garibaldi 27
Trastevere and
Gianicolo ⑦
+39 06 589 6055**

Tucked away on the slope of the Janiculum Hill, this is a great spot to sip on a drink especially during the warmer days, as you can sit at a table on the terrace, surrounded by leafy trees. Plentiful food comes for free with the purchase of a drink during *aperitivo* hour. There's often a DJ set.

153 DRINK KONG

**Piazza di San
Martino ai Monti 8
Colosseum and
San Giovanni** ⑤
+39 06 2348 8666
drinkkong.com

Named tenth best bar in the world by
Le Cocktail Connoisseur in only its third year
of operation. The theme is cyber punk,
inspired by Japan and *Blade Runner,* with
neon lights, arcade games and a bar that
offers bespoke whisky and *sake* tastings.
Located in a former bicycle shop in the
shadow of the 12th-century Torre dei
Capocci, Drink Kong also offers live music
and DJ sets.

154 DOPPIOZEROO

**Via Ostiense 68
Testaccio and
Aventino** ⑧
+39 06 5730 1961
doppiozeroo.com

A place that's good any time of the day,
from breakfast to lunch. But the best
time to head there is around *aperitivo*,
from 6 pm to 9 pm every day, when they
serve a lavish buffet with pasta, pizza,
salads, focaccia, potatoes, and Nutella
bites. Still hungry? Stay for dinner!

155 CORE BISTROT

**Via delle Palme 71-B/F
East Rome** ⑫
+39 06 8892 1996

There's a Zen-like, post-industrial
simplicity to Core: exposed brick walls,
geometric wrought-iron tables with
unfinished wooden tops, lighting fixtures
that look plucked out of a coal mine.
You'd never guess it was a former gambling
house. Cuisine consists of cold antipasti,
with craft beer, wine, and cocktails.

GATSBY CAFÈ

55 PLACES TO SHOP

———

5 beautiful HISTORIC SHOPS ——————— 94

5 cool places to hunt for VINYLS ——————— 96

5 charming places to buy
MUSICAL INSTRUMENTS ——————— 98

5 unusual BOOKSHOPS ——————— 100

5 markets to SHOP LIKE THE LOCALS ——— 102

5 of the best HOME DECOR SHOPS ——————— 104

5 dazzling JEWELLERY shops ——————— 106

5 VINTAGE SHOPS to browse for hours ——————— 108

5 classy SHOPS FOR HIM ——————— 110

5 neat SHOPS FOR HER ——————— 112

5 places to buy
MODERN ANTIQUE FURNITURE ——————— 114

5 beautiful
HISTORIC SHOPS

156 PARALUMI LAR
Via del Leoncino 29
Trident ④
+39 06 687 8175
paralumi.it

Since 1939 the Gualdani family have been hand-making astonishing lampshades, using different materials and techniques, from hand-sewn parchment, to plissé colourful precious fabrics. Here you can buy very refined lamps made of such materials as bronze, iron, wood and ceramics.

157 ANTICA CARTOTECNICA
Piazza dei
Caprettari 61
Centre West ③
+39 06 687 5671
anticacartotecnica.it

If you love writing, this is the place for you: their pen collection – including vintage and contemporary pieces – is quite impressive. Founded in 1930, the shop has maintained a quaint atmosphere. They sell everything from handmade notebooks to customizable stationery paper.

158 SCHOSTAL
Via della Fontanella
di Borghese 29
Trident ④
+39 06 679 1240
schostalroma.com

Originally opened in 1870 in Via del Corso with the name of 'To the city of Vienna, Schostal', it relocated here in 2010, offering the same classic, timeless high-quality products, such as men's cotton shirts, pure Merino wool knitwear, elegant pyjamas, linen andkerchiefs, and silk ties.

159 CALZOLERIA PETROCCHI

Vicolo delle Ceste 29
Centre West ③
+39 06 687 6289
calzoleriapetrocchi.it

A historic atelier which has been designing and handmaking shoes for movie stars, musicians, artists and entrepreneurs, like Sergio Leone, Marcello Mastroianni, Anthony Quinn, and Ennio Morricone. They have a prêt-à-porter line but will also gladly custom-make a pair of shoes.

160 ANTICA MANIFATTURA CAPPELLI

Via degli Scipioni 46
Vatican ②
+39 06 3972 5679
patriziafabrihats.com

In 2003, Patrizia Fabri took over the oldest hat-maker in Rome, founded in 1936. Not much has changed since then. They still employ time-honoured techniques, and use old-fashioned polished wooden molds. In addition to their own handiwork, they also offer items by major international brands, like Stetson, Lock, and Panizza.

156 PARALUMI LAR

5 cool places to hunt for
VINYLS

161 TRE DE TUTTO

Via Giustino
de Jacobis 19
South Rome ⑬
+39 06 8760 6301
tredetuttogarbatella.it

A restaurant where you can pick records to spin in the vinyl corner while you eat your meal. It's a haven for music lovers, so don't expect peace and quiet. The scene is lively, and the food is tasty. What could be better than listening to The Smashing Pumpkins while eating smashed pumpkins? Or, to be more precise, the pumpkin gnocchi with *guanciale* and pecorino cheese.

162 BAR BRUNORI CAFFÈ E VINILE

Largo Chiarini
Giovanni 2
Testaccio and
Aventino ⑧
+39 06 574 6418

Perhaps it's suffering an identity crisis. But you'll love Bar Brunori for never stopping rocking. With the advent of CDs, this record store couldn't keep up. So they added a bar and cafe. Now you can browse Stones and Stooges records while sipping your latte.

163 PORTA PORTESE FLEA MARKET

Piazza Ippolito Nievo
Trastevere and
Gianicolo ⑦

You can find virtually anything at the Porta Portese flea market, including that long-lost record to finish out your Beatles collection. Vinyl vendors usually set up stands close to Piazza Ippolito Nievo, just across from the hot sausage vendors. Records in good to mint condition sell for 10 euro on average.

164 MILLERECORDS

Via Merulana 91
Colosseum and
San Giovanni ⑤
+39 06 7049 0109
millerecords.it

A record store with roots dating back to the 60s, when the founder was DJing parties and started selling vinyls on the side. Since then, Millerecords (Thousands of Records) has become a Roman temple for music enthusiasts, searching for 33s, 45s, and 78s, both new and used, and every thinkable genre.

165 L'ALLEGRETTO DISCHI

Via Oslavia 44
Vatican ②
+39 338 938 2519
lallegrettodischi.
business.site

Opera lovers should make L'Allegretto Dischi their first stop. Their selection is vast, specialising in classical, chamber, choral, Italian, and international jazz, with some 70s-centric rock and pop. They also offer a wide range of cult films on DVD, books and even comic books. Please stay in business!

5 charming places to buy
MUSICAL
INSTRUMENTS

---

166 ROMA LIUTERIA DI MATHIAS MENANTEAU
Via di Santa Maria
Maggiore 150
Colosseum and
San Giovanni ⑤
+39 339 351 7677
romaliuteria.it

French luthier Mathias Menanteau is a one-man-band, dividing his time between restoration, sound adjustment, and construction. His extensive resume includes restoring violins by Stradivarius and Guarnerius del Gesù in Cremona. This workshop, with its medieval arches and a curious cat, is too charming to believe.

167 BANDIERA FRANCO
Via Cavour 145
Colosseum and
San Giovanni ⑤
+39 06 481 8435
bandieramusic.net

This warm and friendly environment offers top-notch customer service, with educated salespeople. Its inventory is all-encompassing, offering Mesa Boogie amps, Taylor guitars, Rode microphones, Zoom recorders, and a variety of eclectic instruments.

168 LA STANZA DELLA MUSICA
Via dei Greci 36
Trident ④
+39 06 321 8874
lastanza
dellamusica.com

La Stanza della Musica stands out for its rich calendar of free concerts and open seminars. Come for the vast selection of instruments, stay for the lecture on lute making, or a solo show by a flamenco guitarist, with wine and finger food.

169 LA CHIAVE DEL VIOLINO

Piazza Lazzaro
Papi 1-B
South Rome ⑱
+39 06 787 244
lachiavedelviolino.it

Opened in 2003, La Chiave del Violino is Rome's top stringed-instrument store, specialising in classical guitars, cellos, violas, basses, and accessories. More than 250 instruments are on display, and some 400 bows, many of which come from local artisans. It also offers a wide selection of music books.

170 LIUTERIA AMERICANA

Via Luciano Manara 5
Trastevere and
Gianicolo ⑦
+39 06 581 0797
romevintage
guitars.com

This vintage guitar shop recalls a clown car – on the outside, it looks tiny; on the inside, it's exploding with rare, must-have instruments and accessories. The inventory includes Fenders, Gibsons, Martins and many other historic brands, dating as far back as the 40s and 50s, depending on availability.

170 LIUTERIA AMERICANA

5 unusual
BOOKSHOPS

171 **GIUFÀ LIBRERIA CAFFÈ**
Via degli Aurunci 38
Centre East ⑥
+39 06 4436 1406
libreriagiufa.it

A funky bookshop/cafe co-op, where you can enjoy a creative panino, while reading Vonnegut. This shop is a hub for the alternative intellectual crowd in the hip San Lorenzo neighbourhood, thanks in part to hosting ongoing events, such as author talks and readings.

172 **OTHERWISE BOOKSHOP**
Via del Governo Vecchio 80
Centre West ③
+39 06 687 9825
otherwisebookstore.com

This independent English-language bookstore stocks thousands of volumes in two rooms, ranging from novels to non-fiction, from children's books to graphic novels, from postcards to notebooks. It also regularly hosts events and meetings with authors and organises reading groups. It's open quite late at night.

173 **IL MARE LIBRERIA INTERNAZIONALE**
Via Leon Battista Alberti 1
Testaccio and Aventino ⑧
+39 347 614 1118
ilmare.com

Opened in 1975, this is, allegedly, the biggest bookstore in the world solely dedicated to books about the sea. Their catalogue includes over 35.000 titles, spanning from the history of navigation to marine biology and recipe books. You can also find maritime maps, boat and ship models, and compasses.

174 IL MUSEO DEL LOUVRE

Via della
Reginella 8-A
Centre West ③
+39 06 6880 7725
ilmuseodellouvre.com

A mix between a bookshop, an art gallery, and a Wunderkammer, the Museo del Louvre is divided in two contiguous spaces: one for the antiques and collectible books, ex-libris, art catalogues, and postcards all dedicated to the historic avantguards of the 20th century, the other for photos. The archive comprises more than 140.000 prints, most of which are vintage.

175 LIBRERIA FAHRENHEIT 451

Piazza Campo
de' Fiori 44
Centre West ③
+39 06 687 5930
libreriafahrenheit451.
wordpress.com

There are still some gems left in the touristy Campo de' Fiori. Libreria Fahrenheit 451 is one of them. Store owners are particularly proud of their books on photography and their rare books, which include a signed edition of *Fahrenheit 451* dedicated to one of them, alongside other editions of Ray Bradbury's dystopian masterpiece.

171 GIUFÀ LIBRERIA CAFFÈ

5 markets to
SHOP LIKE
THE LOCALS

---

176 MERCATO DEI FIORI
Via Trionfale 45
Vatican ②
+39 06 3973 8027

Don't be (too) alarmed by the utter decrepitude of Rome's flower market. With its broken windows and leaky roof, this Fascist-era warehouse stands out in sharp contrast to the beauty of its wares. The prices are impossible to beat – you might find a bouquet of roses for 6 euro. Open only on Tuesday, from 8 am to 1 pm.

177 PIAZZA MAZZINI MARKET
Piazza Giuseppe Mazzini
Vatican ②

An antique market with over 100 different stands devoted to collectibles, vintage clothing, paintings, and handicrafts. It's open the first and third Sunday of every month. From November through January 6 it becomes a Christmas market, offering a wide variety of gifts, including handmade woodcrafts from Italy's Alpine regions.

178 MERCATINO DEL BORGHETTO FLAMINIO

Via Flaminia 32
Centre North ⑨
+39 06 588 0517

This flea market got its start in the 90s, inspired by American garage sales. Vendors tend to be average Joes emptying the home of a deceased loved one, or impoverished college students. The 92-euro vendor's fee ensures a level of quality above what you'd find in an American garage. There's an entry fee of 1,60 euro. Open every Sunday.

179 MERCATO METRONIO

Via Magnagrecia 50
Centre East ⑥

Biodynamic vegetables, vintage clothes, and fresh flowers are all in abundance at the Mercato Metronio, which is worth the visit just for the mid-20th-century architecture. Unveiled by renowned engineer Riccardo Morandi in 1957, the concrete space boasts early spiral car ramps and an unusual, 'pleated' façade. Closed on Sunday.

180 MERCATO NOMENTANO

Piazza Alessandria 1
Centre North ⑨
+39 328 177 4008

This gorgeous covered market was recently restored, bringing back to life its 1920s brickwork, wrought-iron doors, and Liberty reliefs of Sabine women holding fruit and vegetable baskets on their heads. Vendors sell mostly local produce. But you'll also notice a growing number of South Asian vendors specialising in avocados, cilantro and chilis.

5 of the best
HOME DECOR SHOPS

181 **YAKY**
Via di Santa Maria
del Pianto 55
Centre West ③
+39 06 6880 7724
yaky.it

One of Rome's most refined boutique furniture shops, focused on early 20th-century Asian decor. Its tiny front window only has enough room for a few items, including gorgeous Tibetan candles. But hiding downstairs is a sprawling showroom, with everything from ornate Japanese cupboards to minimalistic pre-communist Chinese lounge chairs. The selection is impeccable while the prices are very reasonable.

182 **MIA HOME DESIGN GALLERY**
Via di Ripetta 224
Trident ④
+39 06 9784 1892
galleriamia.it

This gorgeous gallery, which was founded by three women and is hidden behind an imposing entrance, is dedicated to design, mixing more contemporary and experimental pieces with retro-style objects. Here you can often find limited-edition and one-of-a-kind items, by major design brands and emerging talent. You can also select furniture from their catalogue and have it made to your specifications.

183 ASSEMBLEA TESTACCIO

Via Alessandro
Volta 22
Testaccio and
Aventino ⑧
+39 06 574 7696

The cheerful Assemblea Testaccio is managed by two women, one with a background in costume design, the other in architecture. Everything is made in Italy, and the focus is trifold: ceramics and porcelain, textiles, and artwork. Locals know it as the store with all the fish plates.

184 CANDLE STORE

Via Urbana 21
Colosseum and
San Giovanni ⑤
+39 06 9027 3263
candlestore.it

A family-run candle store with items in all shapes, colours and sizes. Every candle is made by hand. Owner and craftswoman Andrea Moraes grew attached to candles growing up in Brazil without electricity. The store also offers courses in candle-making for adults and children.

185 SCENOGRAPHY

Viale Liegi 7-B
Centre North ⑨
+39 06 8535 8945
scenographyroma.com

Where a refurbished tractor seat becomes a stool, and a cast-iron Singer sewing machine is converted into a table. Scenography is your destination for bespoke, vintage furniture with a twist. But the owner Federica also knows when not to do too much, restoring European furniture to their original charm. If any store is going to have that original Vespa sign you've been looking for, this is the place.

5 dazzling
JEWELLERY
shops

186 **PERLEI – GIOIELLI ARTIGIANALI**
Via del Boschetto 35
Trident ④
+39 06 4891 3862
perlei.com

A jewellery store *per lei* (for her), concentrating on minimalist design, with a penchant for the asymmetrical and the modern. Think Alexander Calder, both in terms of shapes and colours. Its location in the delightful Via del Boschetto, surrounded by artisans of all sorts, makes it worth the visit.

187 **ALTERNATIVES GALLERY**
Via della Chiesa Nuova 10
Centre West ③
+39 06 6830 8233
alternatives.it

The minimalist space of this contemporary jewellery store, with its polished concrete floor and metal box displays, would make Donald Judd feel at home. Much of the jewellery is in the same vein. Artists include Satomi Kawai, Karin Roy Andersson, and Gigi Mariani.

188 **CO.RO. JEWELS**
Via della Scrofa 52
Centre West ③
+39 06 4893 0454
corojewels.com

A jewellery shop that specialises in turning works of architecture into wearable art. There's the silver aqueduct bracelet, the golden pantheon ring, and the gold and bronze *gazometro* necklace, based on the gasometer landmark in the Ostiense neighbourhood. Most designs are inspired by Rome or Italian monuments, but not all.

189 MASSIMO MARIA MELIS

Via dell'Orso 57
Centre West ③
+39 06 686 9188
massimo
mariamelis.com

Massimo Maria Melis is a master goldsmith, reinventing the styles and techniques of ancient Greek, Etruscan, and Roman jewellery. Think *Game of Thrones*, though much of his work is surprisingly subtle, even modern. Every detail is painstakingly made by hand. His clients include aristocrats, senior churchmen and celebrities.

190 SOTTOBOSCO

Via Baccina 40
Colosseum and
San Giovanni ⑤
+39 06 4890 6839
sottoboscoshop.it

This tiny space punches above its weight in terms of creativity and surprises. The shop focuses on artisanal jewellery and design from rising European talent, with an emphasis on sustainable materials. Many of the lines they carry feature romantic pieces and some are made in-house.

186 PERLEI

5
VINTAGE SHOPS
to browse for hours

191 TWICE VINTAGE SHOP

Via di San Francesco
a Ripa 7
Trastevere and
Gianicolo ⑦
+39 06 581 6859
twicevintage.com

A hipster haven, with merchandise ranging from rustic Americana to preppy and urban. Brands tend to be denim-heavy, i.e. Levi's, Wrangler, Carhartt, and Lee. There's also a wide variety of name-brand shoes and handbags, mostly leather. The store owners are keenly aware of what's cool.

192 MADEMOISELLE VINTAGE

Via Alberto
da Giussano 62e
East Rome ⑪
+39 06 5272 7686
mademoisellevintage.it

Located in the edgy-trendy neighbour-hood of Pigneto, Mademoiselle Vintage caters to the local hipster clientele with a mixture of hip, secondhand attire and new, handmade wares, like kimonos and lingerie from local artisans. The selection is constantly adapting, and on display at Rome flea markets.

193 SCALA BLU VINTAGE

Via Ascoli Piceno 16
Centre East ⑥
+39 06 701 8733

The name comes from the wooden blue staircase inside, covered in wingtips and studded satchels, leading to a crowded loft space. Every square inch of this minuscule store is covered in retro. The merchandise tends to be in incredibly good condition. Call ahead for business hours.

194 SITENNE

Via Cairoli 55-57
Centre East ⑥
+39 06 7725 0991
sitenne.com

These are professionals. In addition to a huge range of real vintage items of women's and men's clothing and accessories from the 20s to the 80s, Sitenne rents much of its selection – a godsend for models, photographers, and directors. Before you visit, take advantage of their online store, it's one of the best in Rome.

195 DRESS AGENCY

Via Giovanni
Antonio Plana 5-A
Centre North ⑨
+39 06 808 0522

This luxury secondhand clothing shop taps the high-end well that is the Parioli neighbourhood. Louis Vuitton, Dolce & Gabbana, and Tod's are common fare, always in such impeccable condition you'd forget they were used. The store policy is to stock nothing over four years old.

191 TWICE VINTAGE SHOP

5 classy
SHOPS FOR HIM

196 GATSBY CAFÈ

Piazza Vittorio
Emanuele II 106
Colosseum and
San Giovanni ⑤
+39 06 6933 9626
gatsby.cafe

How about sipping on a coffee or a cocktail while shopping for a hat? Dive into the 1950s atmosphere of this charming bistro, a former hat shop called Venturini – it still bears the original neon sign upstairs, integrated in the decor. On the mezzanine floor, to the left, a small room displays a selection of designer hats.

197 MACHETE BARBER SHOP

Via A. Pacinotti 23
Trastevere and
Gianicolo ⑦
+39 06 5538 9352
macheteshop.it

A gleefully hipster chain of barber shops, specialising in creative facial hair. The barbers are the best representation of the store: 20-and 30-somethings with mutton chops, wearing suspenders, with sleeves rolled up so as not to cover their ink. The old-timey interior and vintage chairs are a fun touch.

198 SARTORIA SCAVELLI

Via Sora 19-A
Centre West ③
+39 06 6839 2164
sartoriascavelli.it

This tailor shop offers traditional elegance and originality in detail. Their custom shirts, suits and ties are cut and sewn by hand, and are made from the finest fabrics. Thanks to a partnership with Italian cobbler Cesare Firrao, Scavelli also offers bespoke handmade shoes.

199 CAMPOMARZIO70

Via di Campo
Marzio 70
Trident ④
+39 06 6920 2123
shop.campomarzio70.it

Avant-garde colognes and experimental face lotions are just a few of the items you'll find at this artistic perfume store, which is managed by the same family's fourth generation. Brands include leading international names in the luxury perfume industry, and Italian niche brands such as the historic and iconic Xerjoff V, Casamorati, and I Profumi del Marmo.

200 ALBERTO VALENTINI – RICERCA

Via di Tor di Nona 58
Centre West ③
+39 339 774 8193

Alberto Valentini is known as the Salvador Dalì of ties, with styles ranging from fanciful designs inspired by Kandinsky, to elegant plaids and silks. His atelier, more Wunderkammer than store, is full of paintings, rugs and garments plucked from the belle époque. Valentini is also a full-service tailor.

197 MACHETE BARBER SHOP

5 neat
SHOPS FOR HER

201 MÉTISSAGE ATELIER
Largo del Pallaro 18
Centre West ③
+39 06 6476 0111
metissageatelierblog.
wordpress.com

This tailor's workshop also offers African handcrafted items, such as handbags and jewellery. The Senegalese owner uses gorgeous African wax print fabrics to create colourful custom-tailored models, and, if you wish, you can also buy the fabrics by the metre.

202 BOMBA
Via dell'Oca 39–41
Trident ④
+39 06 361 2881
atelierbomba.com

Extraordinary elegance, with natural fabrics, that fits each client's personality: this is what guides sociologist Cristina Bomba's approach to both the limited edition ready-to-wear items, and the custom-tailored pieces. Great assortment of shoes and refined jewellery as well, also by other designers. Her wedding gowns are bespoke haute couture artworks.

203 PROFUMERIA PARENTI
Via Monte Santo 32
Vatican ②
+39 06 3751 5842
parentiprofumeria.com

This perfumery offers a vast assortment of high-end, traditional and artisanal perfumes together with the best-known more commercial brands. There are also several lines of cosmetics, and beard care products for men.

204 PATTY BLOOM
Via Paganica 9
Centre West ③
+39 06 8377 4148
pattybloom.it

At Italy's first bra-fitting atelier, founders Patrycja Lewicka and Joanna Grunt believe that bras should be comfortable, while enhancing your silhouette. The best way to achieve that is to custom tailor each bra, which they do for every one of their customers.

205 DEL GIUDICE
Via dei Coronari 2
Centre West ③
+39 06 4754 2982
delgiudiceroma.com

Founded in 1959, this family-run leather shop specialises in handmade purses, briefcases, wallets, and belts. You can create your own bag, by selecting the model, perusing the leathers, and picking the colour. If you have a special design in mind, bring your own drawing or photo, and they can turn it into a purse.

201 MÉTISSAGE ATELIER

5 places to buy
MODERN ANTIQUE FURNITURE

---

206 **UNDER THE INFLUENCE**
Via del Polverone 3
Centre West ③
+39 329 561 6131
undertheinfluence.it

In this eclectic gallery, conceived in 2014 by Vittorio Mango, you'll find mostly objects from the 1940s to the 1980s, where equal attention is devoted to design, mid-century modern pieces, and the more classic. Among the featured names are some of the most sought-after American, French and Italian designers, like Adrian Pearsall and Vladimir Kagan.

207 **BINARIO4**
Via di
Monte Verde 53-F
West Rome ⑬
+39 339 623 4077
binario4.jimdo.com

This artisanal workshop is proof that refurbished furniture can often outshine the trendiest new models. If you are looking for something more stylish, Silvana Fantino has a cool selection of French and Piedmontese pieces, and Danish design items from the 1950s–60s–70s.

208 **ALAIN**
Via del Pellegrino 171
Centre West ③
+39 06 6880 7747
alainrome.com

A mix between a shop, a lab, and an atelier, this space offers unique pieces ranging from the 1920s to the 1980s that the owner personally selects and restores, or that he himself produces. From lamps to tables, from chairs to sculptures, the objects here seem to turn into artworks.

209 LAMPS 60

Viale dei Quattro
Venti 47
Trastevere and
Gianicolo ⑦
+39 06 8360 4962
lamps60.com

The name could be somewhat misleading, as there's so much more than just lamps in this 200-sq-metre gallery. Besides lighting, the owners Camilla and Fabrizio propose an ample selection of furniture, chairs, and various objects, dating from the 1950s through the 1970s. Best to book an appointment in advance.

210 RE(F)USE

Via della Fontanella
di Borghese 40
Trident ④
+39 06 6813 6975
carminacampus.com

An experimental and conceptual shop, where everything is created with waste materials that are recycled and reused into new cool objects. Each piece is handmade, mostly by Italian artisans, and comes with a tag explaining its history and provenance.

206. UNDER THE INFLUENCE

HORTI SALLUSTIANI

35 BUILDINGS
TO ADMIRE

———

5 buildings that MATTER IN ART ——————— 118

5 UNEXPECTED FINDS in the city ——————— 121

5 incredible LIBRARIES ——————— 124

5 cool examples of
CONTEMPORARY ARCHITECTURE ——— 126

5 splendid VILLAS ——————— 128

5 places to see
FASCIST-ERA ARCHITECTURE ——————— 130

5 lesser-known CHURCHES not to miss ——————— 132

5 buildings that
MATTER IN ART

---

211 **PALAZZO SACCHETTI**
Via Giulia 66
Centre West ③

A rare example of a palace that's still inhabited by the noble family after which it's named – hence the difficulty in visiting. The interior is frescoed by renowned Renaissance artists such as Francesco Salviati. The garden features a Roman nymphaeum, which would have reached the Tiber. The structure also makes an appearance in Paolo Sorrentino's Oscar-winning *The Great Beauty*. The palazzo can be visited on request.

212 **PALAZZO DELLA CANCELLERIA**
Piazza della Cancelleria 1
Centre West ③
+39 06 6988 7566

The earliest Renaissance palace in Rome. Today it hosts a permanent exhibit on Leonardo Da Vinci and several Holy See tribunals. It was also the reported residence of the late Cardinal Bernard Law, the former Boston archbishop who resigned amid the Catholic Church sex abuse scandal. You need an advance reservation to visit, but you can see part of it with the Leonardo show.

212 PALAZZO DELLA CANCELLERIA

211 PALAZZO SACCHETTI

119

213 PALAZZO MASSIMO ALLE COLONNE – PRIVATE CHAPEL

Corso Vittorio
Emanuele II 141
Centre West ③
+39 06 6880 1545

The convex palazzo façade owes its curved shape to the foundations of the ancient theatre it's built upon. The current structure, which dates back to 1536, includes a private chapel, open only on March 16, from 7 am to 1 pm, to mark when Saint Philip Neri miraculously brought a young boy back to life here on that day.

214 PYRAMID OF CESTIUS

Via Raffaele
Persichetti
Testaccio and
Aventino ⑧
+39 06 3996 7709
coopculture.it/en/poi/
pyramid-of-cestius

When you think of pyramids, you probably think of ancient Egypt. But ancient Rome had them too, and one is still standing, right between Rome's Ostiense and Aventino neighbourhoods. Housing the tomb of the wealthy praetor Gaius Cestius, it was completed around 12 BC. The style was inspired by Cleopatra's time in Rome, and the pyramid was eventually incorporated into the Roman walls.

215 CASINO DELL'AURORA PALLAVICINI

Via XXIV Maggio 43
Trident ④
+39 06 8346 7000
casinoaurora
pallavicini.it

The Renaissance palace that belonged to Cardinal Scipione Borghese, the legendary art collector who gave us the Borghese Gallery and sponsored such baroque icons as Caravaggio and Bernini. The palace's main room, which features Guido Reni's masterpiece fresco L'Aurora, can be seen for free the first day of every month except January (from 10 to 12 am and 3 to 5 pm). Private visits available on request.

5

UNEXPECTED FINDS

in the city

216 **PORTICUS AEMILIA**
Via Rubattino 38
Testaccio and
Aventino ⑧

This massive structure was built between 193 BC and 174 BC. Its function is still debated: given its proximity to the river, it was either used as a warehouse, or as a shelter for warships. This is one of the most ancient examples of tufa being used in *opus incertum*, a masonry technique that uses irregularly cut stone.

217 **HORTI SALLUSTIANI**
Piazza Sallustio 21
Centre North ⑨
+39 06 4201 1597
hortisallustiani.it

The ruins of these landscaped pleasure gardens date back to the first century BC, when they were developed by the Roman historian Sallust (which gives this neighbourhood the name Sallustiano), who acquired the property from Julius Caesar after his death. They fell into decay after the Goths sacked Rome in the 5th century.

216 PORTICUS AEMILIA

218 WALL DRAWING BY SOLDIER

AT: VILLA TORLONIA
Via Nomentana 70
Centre East ⑥
+39 06 0608
museivillatorlonia.it

Like so many aristocratic families in Italy, the Torlonias were big fans of Fascism, so much so they rented Mussolini this villa for just one lira per year. Following World War II, the building was occupied by British soldiers. One of them covered the attic wall of the Casino Nobile with a vivid pastoral scene, including a beautiful bird drawn with pastels.

219 AMPHITHEATRUM CASTRENSE

Piazza di Santa Croce
in Gerusalemme
Centre East ⑥
+39 06 7061 3053
santacroceroma.it

Sometimes called 'Rome's other amphitheatre' after the Colosseum. Only the bottom floor remains of the three-storey structure. A mass animal grave on the premises suggests ancient Romans put on live hunting games here before it was incorporated into the Aurelian Walls.

220 THEATRE OF POMPEY

Via di Grotta Pinta 39
Centre West ③

Wondering why this façade has a concave curve? Until roughly 1500 years ago, this was the seating area of the Theatre of Pompey. The stage would have been behind you. The ruins have dictated the layout for this entire neighbourhood, and are still visible in many nearby restaurants and other businesses built on top of them.

5 incredible
LIBRARIES

221 SOCIETÀ GEOGRAFICA ITALIANA

Via della Navicella 12
Colosseum and
San Giovanni ⑤
+39 06 700 8279
societageografica.net

Boasting some 300.000 volumes, this is one of the most important specialised libraries in the world. Housed inside a 16th-century villa, it includes a section with over 50.000 modern and historical maps, focussing on Italy's territory and seas, and, more than 150.000 photographs from the mid-19th century onwards. Visits on appointment only.

222 BIBLIOTECA CASANATENSE

Via di Sant Ignazio 52
Centre West ③
+39 06 6976 0300
casanatense.
beniculturali.it

Located inside the Gothic cloister of Santa Maria Sopra Minerva, this cathedral of books was founded in 1702 by Dominican friars. Today it holds some 400.000 volumes in wall-to-wall sculpted wooden bookshelves. Free admission upon appointment.

223 VALLICELLIANA

Piazza della Chiesa
Nuova 18
Centre West ③
+39 06 6880 2671
vallicelliana.it

This 16th-century library boasts over 100.000 volumes of antique and ancient manuscripts, incunabula, and books, stacked on two levels of carved wooden bookshelves from the 17th century. The library is part of the Institute of the Oratory of Saint Philip Neri.

224 ACCADEMIA DEI LINCEI

Via della Lungara 10
Trastevere and
Gianicolo ⑦
+39 06 680 271
lincei.it

Founded in 1603, this library was conceived as the nucleus of the Accademia dei Lincei, one of the world's first academies of the scientific revolution. Books collected over the centuries showcase the interdisciplinary spirit of the academy, ranging from philosophy, maths, and science, to literature, alchemy and hermetic texts. Open to the public. Closed in August.

225 ANGELICA

Piazza di
Sant'Agostino 8
Centre West ③
+39 06 684 0801
bibliotecaangelica.
cultura.gov.it

The library owes its name to Angelo Rocca, the 16th-century bishop who managed the Vatican printing house, helping him amass a collection of 20.000 volumes. Today the collection is roughly ten times as large, consisting of liturgical and scholarly books, maps, and atlases, as well as four Renaissance globes.

223 VALLICELLIANA

5 cool examples of
CONTEMPORARY ARCHITECTURE

---

226 CHIESA DEL SANTO VOLTO DI GESÙ

Via della
Magliana 162
West Rome ⑬
+39 06 550 1063
parrocchiasantovolto.it

Rome's outer neighbourhoods are plagued by modern churches that can only be described as architectural monstrosities. This, however, is not one of them. With its hyper futurism, solid-white interior, and apsidal window recalling a vortex, you'd be forgiven for mistaking this church for the set of a science-fiction film.

227 BRITISH EMBASSY

Via Venti
Settembre 80-A
Centre North ⑨

In 1946, a terrorist attack destroyed Villa Bracciano, where the British Embassy was located. Sir Spence was called to design the new building. The functional, brutalist embassy was one of the most controversial works of architecture of its time, because of its avant-garde appearance, which was in stark contrast with the Porta Pia gate, in the Aurelian Walls, by Michelangelo.

228 LA LANTERNA

AT: H&M
Via Tomacelli 157
Trident ④
+39 06 6937 7739
lalanternarome.com

Composed of triangular panels of glass, this lantern-like glass sculpture juts vertically through the middle of the H&M store and erupts on the roof. The work by famed Roman architect Massimiliano Fuksas lights up kaleidoscopically at night.

229 LA CHIESA DEL DIO PADRE MISERICORDIOSO

Piazza Largo Terzo
Millennio 8
East Rome ⑫
+39 06 231 5833

Designed by American 'starchitect' Richard Meier, the Jubilee Church stands out for its giant concrete sails reaching over 30 metres into the sky. Its white colour, made by adding Carrara marble and titanium dioxide to the mixture, is a trademark of Meier's other work, such as the Getty Center in Los Angeles.

230 MAXXI

Via Guido Reni 4-A
Centre North ⑨
+39 06 320 1954
maxxi.art

Rome's pre-eminent contemporary art museum, exhibiting works by 21st-century artists such as Alighiero Boetti, Francesco Clemente, William Kentridge, Mario Merz, and Gerhard Richter. The futuristic building itself, designed by late starchitect Zaha Hadid, is reason enough to pay a visit. There's a sprawling outdoor space that's great for kids to run around and play in.

228 LA LANTERNA

5 splendid
VILLAS

231 VILLA MASSIMO

Largo di Villa
Massimo 1–2
Centre East ⑥
+39 06 4425 931
villamassimo.de/it

Formerly a suburban estate of the aristocratic Massimo family, the villa was one of the grandest in the area, with grounds stretching over 60 acres before the onset of 20th-century urban sprawl. It currently hosts the German Academy, which sponsors residencies for that country's top artists.

232 VILLA LANTE

Passeggiata del
Gianicolo 10
Trastevere and
Gianicolo ⑦
+39 06 6880 1674
irfrome.org

A summer house designed by Giulio Romano, the star pupil of Raphael, whose Mannerist touch is visible in the lightness this villa possesses. Interior frescoes are by Raphael's workshop. Visitors welcome Monday to Friday from 9 to 12 am. Must be booked in advance.

233 VILLA OF THE QUINTILII

Via Appia Nuova 1092
East Rome ⑫
+39 06 712 9121
+39 06 3996 7700
*parcoarcheologico
appiaantica.it/luoghi*

So massive are these ruins that locals once mistook them for an ancient cityscape as opposed to the stately property of 2nd-century Roman consuls. Today the site has a museum, nymphaeum, tepidarium, and a grand terrace with a commanding view of the Castelli Romani.

234 **VILLA MARAINI**
BY APPOINTMENT ONLY
Via Ludovisi 48
+39 06 420 421
Trident ④
istitutosvizzero.it

It would be one of Rome's finest baroque buildings, were it not built at the start of the 20th century for a Swiss industrialist. The tower offers one of the highest and unobstructed views of the city. Today the villa is the headquarters of the Swiss Institute. Admission is 5 euro, or free during select lectures and events.

235 **VILLA PAPALE DELLA MAGLIANA**
Via Luigi Ercole Morselli 13
West Rome ⑬
+39 06 655 961

A glorified papal hunting lodge, the Castello, as it's nicknamed for its crenellated roofline, was beloved by Leo X, a Medici pope and avid huntsman. He hired Raphael's workshop to adorn the inner chapel with frescoes, and the hall of the villa itself with grotesque imagery. The hunting grounds have long been consumed by urban sprawl. Calling ahead for visit times is highly recommended.

232 **VILLA LANTE**

5 places to see

FASCIST-ERA ARCHITECTURE

---

236 TEATRO PALLADIUM

Piazza Bartolomeo
Romano 8
South Rome ⑭
+39 06 5733 2772
*teatropalladium.
uniroma3.it*

Completed in 1931 by Innocenzo
Sabbatini, this is the symbolic entrance
to the working-class Garbatella neighbourhood. The hemisphere-shaped
ground floor is a theatre, owned by the
Roma Tre university, while the upper
stories are residential, crowned by a neo-
classical loggia that gives the structure
a monumental presence.

237 PALAZZO DELLE POSTE

Via Marmorata 4
Testaccio and
Aventino ⑧
+39 06 5701 8228

While said not to be a steadfast Fascist,
Adalberto Libera is one of the architects
most associated with the movement,
thanks in no small part to the Palazzo
delle Poste, which still functions as a post
office today. Mussolini presided over the
opening in 1935, an important year for
Rome architecture. Its brutal geometry
pairs peculiarly well with the 12 BC
Pyramid of Cestius just across the street.

238 L'EDIFICIO POSTALE ROMA NOMENTANO

Piazza Bologna 39
Centre East ⑥
+39 06 4411 6229

One of the most important architectural works of Italian rationalism. Unveiled in 1935 by architect Mario Ridolfi, the structure sticks out for its double-curved travertine-plated façade. The bulbousness continues indoors, seen in the rounded edges of the ceiling, much of which is obstructed by modern postal fixtures.

239 LA SAPIENZA UNIVERSITY

Piazzale Aldo Moro 5
Centre East ⑥
+39 06 49911
uniroma1.it

A Fascist interpretation of international Modernism, by architect Marcello Piacentini, who built the structure in 1935 with the latest construction techniques, yet clad it in travertine to lend it a classical Roman look. Note its similarity in style to the EUR neighbourhood, but drastically smaller scale.

240 ACCADEMIA DI SCHERMA – CASA DELLE ARMI

Viale delle Olimpiadi 60
Aurelio ①

On the far south side of the Foro Italico, you'll find the historic fencing academy, a masterpiece of Italian Rationalism, however one that's undergone significant neglect and alteration, acting once as a makeshift courtroom, and later a police station. It currently serves the Italian Olympic committee, and opens sporadically for special events.

5 lesser-known
CHURCHES
not to miss

241 SAN GREGORIO MAGNO AL CELIO

Piazza di San
Gregorio al Celio 1
Colosseum and
San Giovanni ⑤
+39 06 700 8227

Named after Pope Saint Gregory I, who sent the church prior, Saint Augustine, to evangelise England in 597, launching the first large-scale mission from Rome to convert pagans to Christianity. Of note is its peristyle forecourt. In the 1970s, Mother Teresa established a food kitchen for the poor in an annexe, which is still operative.

242 SANT'ONOFRIO AL GIANICOLO

Piazza di
Sant'Onofrio 2
Trastevere and
Gianicolo ⑦
+39 06 686 4498

A mecca for medieval poetry scholars, this is where Torquato Tasso spent his remaining years and died in 1595, several years after publishing his famous *Jerusalem Delivered*. Today the church houses his museum, manuscripts, and his death mask. The easiest and most scenic way to get there is via a medieval staircase from the Lungotevere.

243 MAUSOLEUM OF SANTA COSTANZA

Via Nomentana 349
Centre North ⑨
+39 06 8620 5456
santagnese.net

A 4th-century circular church in excellent condition. Scholars differ on the mausoleum's primary occupant: long believed to be its namesake Saint Constance, recent research indicates it's more likely Helena, the wife of Emperor Julian. Both were daughters of Emperor Constantine. The well-preserved mosaics, with both Christian and pagan motifs, are particularly noteworthy.

244 BASILICA DI SANTI NEREO E ACHILLEO

Via delle Terme
di Caracalla 28
Testaccio and
Aventino ⑧
+39 335 401 789
vallicella.org

The 4th-century church is dedicated to Nereus and Achilleus, Roman soldiers who were martyred after converting to Christianity, and whose bodies were buried here. The unassuming façade belies an interior that's resplendent with early Renaissance frescoes and ancient Roman spoglia from the nearby baths of Caracalla.

245 CHIESA DI SAN SABA

Piazza Gian Lorenzo
Bernini 20
Testaccio and
Aventino ⑧
+39 06 6458 0140
sansaba.gesuiti.it

Founded in the 7th century by monks fleeing their monastery of Saint Sabas in Palestine, which was under Islamic invasion. In the 8th century it served as a jail for Antipope Constantine II. Artistically, it's noteworthy for its Byzantine, cruciform structure, and interior frescoes depicting the miracles of Saint Nicolas.

THE TOMBS OF VIA LATINA

75 PLACES
TO DISCOVER
ROME

5 routes to see **A DIFFERENT ROME** —————— 138

5 **MAGIC OR LEGENDARY** places —————— 140

5 hidden **SUNDIALS OR MERIDIANS** —————— 142

5 interesting **FOUNTAINS** —————— 144

5 amazing **PARKS** —————— 146

5 surprising **GARDENS** and
COURTYARDS —————— 148

5 places to **WATCH THE WORLD** go by —————— 150

5 **BURIAL SITES** to visit —————— 152

5 occupied **SOCIAL CENTRES** —————— 154

5 spots for **CALCIO LOVERS** —————— 156

5 places where **TIME AND SPACE**
are measured —————— 158

5 *places to explore the* HISTORY
OF MEDICINE ———————————————— 161

5 UNDERGROUND *sites you should see* ——————— 163

5 *places from* WWII HISTORY ——————————— 165

5 NON-CATHOLIC *sites* ——————————————— 168

5 routes to see
A DIFFERENT ROME

246 **CLIVO DI SCAURO**

Colosseum and
San Giovanni ⑤

An arcaded walkway that begins at the church of San Gregorio al Celio, running beneath the buttresses of the Basilica of Saints John and Paul. In ancient Rome it stretched much farther, branching off from the road that connected the Colosseum to the Circus Maximus through the dip between the Caelian and Palatine hills.

247 **WALK UP MONTE MARIO**

Entrances from
Piazzale Maresciallo
Giardino, Viale del
Parco Mellini
Aurelio ①

Need to get your head above the smog line? Monte Mario is the highest hill in Rome, though not one of the 'Seven Hills' as it's outside the ancient city limits. This natural reserve offers a momentary escape from the urban jungle for joggers, birdwatchers, and even stargazers, hence the nearby observatory.

248 CLIVO DI ROCCA SAVELLA

Testaccio and
Aventino ⑧

Once the main access road to the Aventine Hill, this ancient footpath is easy to miss coming from ground level. It's best approached from the top, near the entrance to the Giardino delle Arance. On the way down, it offers some of the most dramatic views of the Tiber River and the southern side of the centre.

249 TRAMLINE 3

Testaccio and
Aventino ⑧

Grab a window seat and enjoy the views of some of Rome's greatest attractions, all for just 1,50 euro. From the south end, a good starting point is along the Via Marmorata. Heading towards Valle Giulia, you'll ride past the Pyramid of Caius Cestius, Circus Maximus, the Palatine, and the Colosseum.

250 BUS LINE 81

Colosseum and
San Giovanni ⑤

The whole route from Piazza Venezia to Via Santo Stefano Rotondo is a visual pleasure, passing four of the seven hills of Rome. After Teatro Marcello, the bus turns at Circus Maximus, just where visitors can enter the ruins of that stadium. At the Colosseum it turns around the Coelian Hill and continues to Via Santo Stefano Rotondo and beyond.

5
MAGIC OR LEGENDARY
places

---

251 PORTA ALCHEMICA

Piazza Vittorio
Emanuele II
Colosseum and
San Giovanni ⑤

Nestled in a corner of the park in Piazza Vittorio, the door flanked by two stone dwarves is all that remains of the 17th-century villa of Marquis Massimiliano Palombara. He's said to have covered the door in esoteric writings left behind by an alchemist who vanished in the night after turning a herb into gold.

252 MIRACULOUS WELL IN THE CHURCH OF SANTA MARIA IN VIA LATA

Via del Corso 306
Centre West ③
+39 06 6989 6465
cryptavialata.it

'Little Lourdes', or the chapel of Madonna del Pozzo, is inside this church on the left. Once the location of a cardinal's stables, this well overflowed in the 13th century, nearly carrying away a painting on stone of the Virgin Mary, which the cardinal rescued and enshrined. Visitors can drink the water.

253 PALAZZO FALCONIERI

Via Giulia 1
Centre West ③
+39 06 6889 6700

Francesco Borromini is the likely author behind the alchemical symbols that mark Palazzo Falconieri. The name means 'falconers', hence the falcon motif inside and outside. Today the building hosts the Hungarian Academy.

254 THE SCAR OF ROLAND'S SWORD

Vicolo della Spada d'Orlando
Centre West ③

Head down this small street off the Pantheon with your eyes peeled at ankle level, and you'll find a marble stump with a conspicuous split down one side. Legend has it that Roland, Charlemagne's chief Paladin, slashed his indestructible sword Durendal against it while fending off a group of Roman knights.

255 POPE JOAN

Corner of Via dei Querceti and Via Santi Quattro Coronati
Colosseum and San Giovanni ⑤

Here stands a neglected oratory with a poorly preserved painting. While certainly a classic rendition of the Madonna with Child, the story goes that it's actually a depiction of the apocryphal Pope Joan, the 9th-century 'Papessa' who masqueraded as a man, fell in love with a cardinal, and gave birth in the middle of the street during a procession.

251 PORTA ALCHEMICA

5 hidden
SUNDIALS OR MERIDIANS

---

256 CASTEL SANT'ANGELO

Lungotevere
Castello 50
Vatican ②
+39 06 681 9111
castelsantangelo.com

In the central parapet of Castel Sant'Angelo, just above the bridge by the same name, there's a sundial etched on the stone balustrade overlooking the Tiber River. It's believed to have been used to synchronise a mechanical clock that used to rest just above this opening until the castle was restored in 1901.

257 COPPEDÈ

Piazza Mincio
Centre North ⑨

Art Nouveau and Tolkien had a baby: Coppedè. Architect Gino Coppedè built this district around Piazza Mincio, marked by a fountain with frogs spitting water. Surrounding residences are frescoed in mythological themes. Among the most eye-catching is Villino delle Fate, with a weather vane on top, and a sundial on the side.

258 TWO ON ONE CORNER

Via Giovanni Battista
Morgagni 23-B
Centre East ⑥

On the two buildings on the corner of Via Morgagni and Viale Margherita, there are two sundials, one eastern declining indicating the hours of the morning, the other western declining, indicating the afternoon hours. The one facing Via Morgagni bears the signs of the zodiac.

259 SANTA MARIA DEGLI ANGELI E DEI MARTIRI

Piazza della Repubblica
Colosseum and San Giovanni ⑤
+39 06 488 0812
santamariadegli angeliroma.it

Commissioned by Pope Clement XI to assert the supremacy of the Gregorian calendar, the bronze diagonal line cuts across the floor of the basilica just before the apse, marking the meridian that crosses Rome. Everyday at solar noon, the sun shines through a small hole in the wall casting a sun-shaped beam on the line.

260 HOROLOGIUM AUGUSTI

Via di Campo Marzio 48
Trident ④

Augustus' Sundial, or what's left of its original platform, is accessed via the basement of this private property, after calling ahead. It originally spanned 160 × 75 metres. The Egyptian obelisk that now stands in Piazza di Montecitorio was its gnomon that casts a shadow on the centre of the Ara Pacis every September 23rd, Augustus' birthday.

259 SANTA MARIA DEGLI ANGELI E DEI MARTIRI

5 interesting
FOUNTAINS

___

261 FONTANA DEI LIBRI
Via degli Staderari
Centre West ③

One of the city's most whimsical fountains, believed to honour the nearby La Sapienza university in its travertine depiction of books gushing water around a stag's head, the symbol of the surrounding district of Sant'Eustachio and the nearby titular church.

262 FONTANA DEL PRIGIONE
Via Goffredo Mameli, intersection with Via Luciano Manara
Trastevere and Gianicolo ⑦

This fountain was built in 1580 by Domenica Fontana, and was originally part of a villa garden on the Esquiline that no longer exists. It gets its name, 'Prison Fountain', from the carving of a prisoner with his hands tied in the central niche. A restoration in 2006 brought out relief carvings of garlands and lion heads.

263 FONTANA DEL MONTE DI PIETÀ
Piazza del Monte di Pietà
Centre West ③

An early-17th-century fountain crowned with an eagle and flanked by two dragons. Both animals make up the coat of arms of Rome's notorious Borghese family. Beneath the eagle is a mask, at the centre of a triangular frieze, spewing water into the basin below. The restored palazzo del Monte di Pietà is worth a gander.

264 FONTANA DELL'ACQUA ACETOSA

Via Enrico Elia
Centre North ⑨

The fountain gets its name from the iron-laden spring that flowed here off the Tiber River. Commemorated in the fountain plaque, Pope Paul V revered its therapeutic qualities and thus commissioned the fountain in 1619, drawing large queues for centuries, until the city deemed the water unsafe in 1959, replacing its source with running water.

265 FONTANA ABBEVERATOIO IN LUNGOTEVERE AVENTINO

Lungotevere
Aventino 5
Testaccio and
Aventino ⑧

It's the only one if this kind that has survived in the city centre. It was originally placed closer to the fountain of the tritons, in front of the temple of Hercules Victor, and was used as a source to provide drinking water to animals. Built in 1717 by Carlo Bizzaccheri, it was moved to its current location after 1870.

264 FONTANA DELL'ACQUA ACETOSA

262 FONTANA DEL PRIGIONE

5 amazing
PARKS

266 **PARCO DEGLI SCIPIONI**

Via di Porta Latina 10
Colosseum and
San Giovanni ⑤
+39 06 0608
sovraintendenza
roma.it

This park used to be an ancient burial ground. The most noteworthy tombs are those of Pomponius Hylas, from the Flavian period, and of the famous Scipio family. The latter dates to the 3rd century BC. It was lost and forgotten until the 18th century, hence its good state of preservation. Call ahead to access the tombs.

267 **VILLA SCIARRA**

Viale delle Mura
Gianicolensi 11
Trastevere and
Gianicolo ⑦
+39 06 0608

A little-known park in the shadow of Villa Doria Pamphilj. What it lacks in size it makes up for in shady trees, ubiquitous benches, and unobstructed views. Its lavish fountains also make it a popular spot for dog walkers and flies in the summer months.

268 **VILLA CELIMONTANA**

Via della Navicella,
Piazza SS. Giovanni
e Paolo
Colosseum and
San Giovanni ⑤

The leafy gardens cover most of the dip between the Caelian and Aventine hills. History runs deep on the grounds. In the 1st century it was a base for Roman firefighters. In the 16th it was obtained by the powerful Mattei family, who built the villa, which now houses the Italian Geographic Society.

269 PARCO DELLA CAFFARELLA

Via della Caffarella
South Rome ⑭
+39 340 006 2218
caffarella.it

An idyllic blend of archeology and nature. The Caffarella Park is off the Appian Way, which accounts for the concentration of ancient Roman tombs. They were commonly used to store hay and grains in the Middle Ages. The 10th-century church of Sant'Urbano was built on top of a temple thought to honour Bacchus.

270 PARCO TORRE DEL FISCALE

Via dell'Acquedotto
Felice 120
East Rome ⑫
+39 06 761 2966
torredelfiscale.it

The park gets its name from its medieval tower. Other landmarks include six Roman aqueducts, plus one from the Renaissance, a series of tombs, and architectural ruins from Imperial Rome. The Casale Museum on the grounds is worth a visit, as is its restaurant, which uses ingredients grown in the park.

267 VILLA SCIARRA

269 PARCO DELLA CAFFARELLA

5 surprising
GARDENS *and*
COURTYARDS

---

271 **BOSCO PARRASIO**

Salita del
Bosco Parrasio
Trastevere and
Gianicolo ⑦
+39 06 6840 8048
*accademia
dellarcadia.it*

The same designer who gave us the Spanish Steps created this beautiful garden. Antonio Canevari built it on three levels connected by staircases running down this hillside. It's the former home of the Accademia dell'Arcadia, a literary academy that would hold readings in the theatre on the upper level.

272 **PALAZZO MATTEI DI GIOVE**

Via Michelangelo
Caetani 32
Centre West ③
+39 06 6840 6901
icbsa.it

The extravagant courtyard, designed by Carlo Maderno, holds excavated ancient Roman artefacts and Late Renaissance pieces side-by-side. Over the years numerous historical figures have resided in the palace, from the artist Caravaggio to the writer Giacomo Leopardi. Today the building houses, among others, the Centre for American Studies, and the Library of Modern and Contemporary History.

273 PALAZZO SANTACROCE

Piazza Benedetto
Cairoli 6
Centre West ③
+39 06 0725 59110
+39 06 684 921

A 15th-century palace with a stone-studded façade, currently the home of the Italian-Latin American Institute. It once belonged to the Santacroce family, powerful tobacco magnates. For a time, tobacco was known in Italy as 'Santacroce herb'. The small, elegant garden can be visited Monday to Friday upon request.

274 SAN SALVATORE IN LAURO

Piazza di San
Salvatore in Lauro 15
Centre West ③
+39 06 687 5187
sansalvatoreinlauro.org

Dating back to the 7th century, the church was rebuilt after a 16th century fire, giving it the cupola, belfry and sacristy. The bright interior is one of architect Ottaviano Mascherino's great achievements. But it's inside the adjacent convent of San Giorgio where we find the understated and peaceful Renaissance cloister.

275 PALAZZO ORSINI TAVERNA

Via di Monte
Giordano 36
Centre West ③
+39 06 683 3785
aldobrandini.it

Once a medieval fortress, it was turned into noble residences where figures such as writer Torquato Tasso resided in the 16th century. In the 19th century the palace was acquired by the Taverna counts of Milan, who still own it today. A large vaulted entranceway leads to a grand courtyard with a 17th-century fountain fed by the Acqua Paola aqueduct.

5 places to
WATCH THE WORLD
go by

---

276 TRAM DEPOT TESTACCIO

Via Marmorata 13
Testaccio and
Aventino ⑧
+39 06 575 4406

A full-service cocktail bar inside a decommissioned tram car, just off one of the city's main tram lines. Covered seating is outdoors, making this an ideal summer spot, under the shade of cherry blossoms. Food such as panini and chocolate cake are served on small cutting boards.

277 TREEBAR

Via Flaminia 226
Centre North ⑨
+39 06 4977 3501
treebar.it

As the name suggests, this cafe sits under the slender patch of trees that divides the Via Flaminia. Its geometric wooden structure feels more Danish than Roman. The large patio is a favourite cocktail spot among the well-dressed en route to the nearby Auditorium Parco della Musica.

278 VILLA ALDOBRANDINI

Via Mazzarino 11
Trident ④
+39 06 0608
sovraintendenza roma.it

An elevated garden with camellias and lemon trees that sits blissfully nearly 100 steps above the noisy Via Nazionale. This vantage gives good views of Trajan's Market, the Quirinale Palace, and the Salita del Grillo walkway. The garden, with its statues and fountain, is the only part of the villa that you can visit.

279 100% BIO

Piazza di Porta
San Paolo 6
Testaccio and
Aventino ⑧
+39 06 574 7778
centopercento.bio

The perfect place for a healthy, delicious, and ethically sourced meal. They'll even give you a discount if you show up on your bicycle. You pay by the pound to eat at the vegetarian buffet. The sun-drenched patio facing the ruins of Porta San Paolo and the Pyramid of Cestius is always abuzz with local colour.

280 PIAZZA SAN COSIMATO

Trastevere and
Gianicolo ⑦

The real heart of Trastevere, where locals still outnumber tourists, and where stores are more genuine. Come before lunch to see the bustling open-air market, flanked by a child-packed playground. In the summertime, expect to see outdoor screenings of independent films and international football matches.

276 TRAM DEPOT TESTACCIO

5
BURIAL SITES
to visit

---

281 POUSSIN'S TOMB
AT: BASILICA DI SAN
LORENZO IN LUCINA
Piazza di San Lorenzo
in Lucina 16-A
Trident ④
+39 06 687 1494

The leading artist of the French Baroque, Nicolas Poussin, spent most of his life in Rome. This marble monument depicts his bust as well as a reproduction of his iconic painting Arcadian Shepherds, which shows herdsmen from antiquity crowding around a tomb – an artistic hall of mirrors if there ever was one.

282 TOMB OF ELIO CALLISTIO OR 'THE DEVIL'S CHAIR'
Piazza Elio Callistio
Centre North ⑨

It's thought to be the tomb of freed Roman slave Elio Callistio. Its nickname, the Devil's Chair, came about in the Middle Ages due to its resemblance, after centuries of decay, to a bishop's chair, and the prostitutes who gathered there. According to local lore, the devil would sit on the chair with his back to the Vatican.

283 COLUMBARIUM OF POMPONIUS HYLAS
Via di Porta Latina 14
Colosseum and
San Giovanni ⑤
+39 06 0608
sovraintendenzaroma.it

Accessed via the Parco degli Scipioni, this underground tomb on the Appian Way is roughly 2000 years old. Yet its rich decoration of mosaics, paintings and stucco is remarkably intact, owing to the fact that it wasn't uncovered until the 19th century.

284 THE TOMBS OF VIA LATINA

Via dell'Arco di
Travertino 151
East Rome ⑫
+39 06 3996 7700
parcoarcheologico
appiaantica.it

Marvellous, well-preserved tombs from the 2nd century less than 6,5 km from the centre of Rome, off the ancient Roman Latina Way, which used to wind for over 160 km inland and south of Rome. Traces of the original basalt road are still visible at the park, along with tombs such as the Sepulchre of the Valerii with its prominent portico.

285 HYPOGEUM OF THE AURELII

Via Luigi Luzzatti 2
Centre East ⑥
+39 06 446 5610
(book in advance)
turismoroma.it/en/
places/ipogeo-degli-
aureli

An underground burial chamber from the 3rd century with both Christian and pagan frescoes, leading scholars to postulate that the Aurelia family, its owners from Imperial Rome, had syncretistic or Gnostic beliefs. Discovered in 1919 during construction of a body shop, the hypogeum was restored with lasers in 2011.

281 POUSSIN'S TOMB

SOCIAL CENTRES

286 CSOA FORTE PRENESTINO

Via Federico
Delpino 187
East Rome ⑫
+39 06 2180 7855
forteprenestino.net

Social centres in Italy are counter-culture squats that tend to host concerts and other cultural activities. Consider Forte Prenestino the Vatican of such. Since this massive defunct military fort was occupied in the 80s it has hosted a regular agenda of exhibits, tastings, and you name it in its numerous underground tunnels and chambers.

287 CASETTA ROSSA

Via Federico
Delpino 187
East Rome ⑫
+39 06 8936 0511
casettarossa.org

Social centres can feel post-apocalyptic, designed in shabby protest against the orderly capitalist dystopia that is the modern condition. Consider Casetta Rossa (Little Red House) a charming gateway drug, offering breakfast, lunch and dinner, in addition to community programs and live music on its leafy terrace.

288 CAGNE SCIOLTE

Via Ostiense 137
South Rome (14)
+39 398 980 8055
(domestic violence
hotline)
cagnesciolte.
noblogs.org

Cagne Sciolte (Bitches Unleashed) is
a feminist social centre that organises
workshops on crafts such as soapmaking,
protests against gender and sexual
discrimination, and plays promoting
women's rights, with vegetarian meals
available. They also offer support for
victims of domestic violence.

289 100CELLE APERTE

Via delle Resede 5
East Rome (12)
100celleaperte.
wordpress.com

100celle Aperte focuses on musical
performance, with recital and practice
rooms, plus a recording studio. Live
music, from classical to folk and jazz,
is the norm. It also has a non-profit
vegetarian co-op grocery, vegan meals
at select events, a wholesale winebar,
and a bike-repair co-op.

290 ACROBAX

Via della
Vasca Navale 6
South Rome (14)
acrobax.org

Founded in 2002 by 'precarious workers',
i.e. labourers with short-term contracts,
who converted an abandoned dog track
into an events space. Bars serve local
beers, stages put on live music, artists put
on cool exhibitions. They even have their
own basketball and rugby matches.

5 spots for
CALCIO LOVERS

---

291 GIANT MURAL OF FRANCESCO TOTTI

Via Apulia 31
Colosseum and
San Giovanni ⑤

It's fitting that in a city famous for street art and its love for calcio you would find a giant mural of Francesco Totti, Rome's football demigod who retired in 2017 at 40+ from captaining AS Roma. Known as 'Il Gladiatore', Totti is easily one of the city's most beloved figures – except among hardcore Lazio fans.

292 ROMA SHOP

Via Leone IV 55
Vatican ②
+39 06 3974 5679
romashop.org

Your one-stop shop for everything AS Roma, including vintage jerseys. They even have special edition Roma New Balance tennis shoes. Prices vary from 19 euro for the newspaper from the day Roma won the national championship in 2001, to 450 euro for Gabriel Omar Batistuta's original jersey.

293 FOUR GREEN FIELDS

Via Silvio
Pellico 18-20-22
Vatican ②
+39 06 372 5091
fourgreenfields.it

This Irish pub draws boisterous crowds, especially during football and rugby matches when Italy plays Ireland. Here you can count on generous pours of Guinness, and surprisingly cocktails as well. The gin and tonic is especially worth the investment.

294 CAMPO TESTACCIO

Via Nicola Zabaglia 31
Testaccio and
Aventino ⑧

The actual stadium was demolished in 2011, and now you can barely see this football field through the towering weeds. It had four wooden seating sections, painted red and yellow, for 20.000 fans. The grounds even included housing for the coach.

295 FONDAZIONE GABRIELE SANDRI

Piazza della Libertà 15
Vatican ②
+39 06 3260 9079

In 2007, Rome police accidentally killed an innocent fan, Gabriele 'Gabo' Sandri, while attempting to quell violence between Lazio and Juventus fans. The foundation was established to promote good sportsmanship. It also houses a public library of international scholarship devoted entirely to football.

291 GIANT MURAL OF FRANCESCO TOTTI

5 places where
TIME AND SPACE
are measured

---

296 CANNON AT THE JANICULUM HILL

Piazzale Giuseppe Garibaldi
Trastevere and Gianicolo ⑦

You can set your watch by the sound of cannon fire every day at noon at the Gianicolo Hill. The tradition dates back to 1847, when Pope Pius XI ordered the city's hundreds of churches to stop chiming their bell towers virtually at random, which they had been doing for centuries.

297 WATER CLOCK ON THE PINCIAN HILL

Viale dell'Orologio
Centre North ⑨

Near the entrance of the Pincio promenade you'll come across a transparent clock tower with water flowing through its innards, splish-sploshing into two canisters at alternating intervals, giving the clock its tic and toc. It's the ingenious late-19th-century handiwork of Dominican friar Giovan Battista Embriaco.

298 MILIARIUM AUREUM

AT: FORUM ROMANUM
Via della Salara Vecchia 5-6
Colosseum and San Giovanni ⑤

All roads lead to Rome. And they all end at the Miliarium Aureum, or 'Golden Milestone', which marked their specific terminus near the Temple of Saturn in the Roman Forum. Remains of its suspected base are labeled here. Scholars suspect markers would have pointed towards major cities and marked their travel time.

296 **CANNON AT THE JANICULUM HILL**

297 **WATER CLOCK ON THE PINCIAN HILL**

299 CALENDAR AT THE BASILICA DI SANTA MARIA MAGGIORE

Piazza di Santa
Maria Maggiore 42
Colosseum and
San Giovanni ⑤

Before there was a church on these grounds, there was a Roman patrician estate from the 2nd or 3rd century, surrounded by a long wall. On it were frescoes of an agricultural calendar. Only the traces from the months of September, October, and November remain. It's the oldest surviving calendar of its kind.

300 THE OCULUS

AT: THE PANTHEON
Piazza della Rotonda
Centre West ③

The Pantheon might be looked at as one of the biggest sundials in Rome. The circular opening on the top of the building (oculus) is the only source of light, and it might have meaningful connections with the solstices and the equinoxes. During the summer solstice, a beam of light projects a huge disk on the ground, with a diametre of 7,8 m, similar to that of the oculus. On April 21st, the 'birthday' of Rome, the sun illuminates the entry of the temple at 12 pm, which would have allowed the emperor to enter in all of his glory.

5 places to explore the
HISTORY
OF MEDICINE

---

301 TEMPLE OF AESCULAPIUS
AT: TIBER ISLAND
Via Ulisse
Aldrovandi 6
Centre West ③

The Senate built this temple to the Greek god of medicine when the plague hit Rome in the 3rd century BC. According to legend, a mythical snake slithered off a ship carrying a statue of Aesculapius from Greece to Rome, to this point on the northern bank of the Tiber Island.

302 ANTICA FARMACIA – SPEZIERIA DI SANTA MARIA DELLA SCALA
Piazza della Scala 23
Trastevere and
Gianicolo ⑦
+39 06 580 6233

This well-preserved antique pharmacy on the first floor of the Carmelitani Scalzi Convent originally carried medicinal herbs cultivated and used by the resident friars. In the 17th century it was opened to the public and used by the Vatican's top doctors. Call ahead to schedule a visit.

303 MUSEO DI STORIA DELLA MEDICINA
Viale dell'
Università 34
Centre East ⑥
+39 06 4991 4766
web.uniroma1.it/
museostoriamedicina

The fascinating Museum of the History of Medicine inside La Sapienza University covers prehistoric to modern times, but concentrates on Egyptian, Greek, and Roman medicine. Exhibits range from artefacts of animal teeth used for dentures in ancient Italy, to medieval casts and Renaissance alchemy laboratories.

304 COMPLEX OF SANTO SPIRITO IN SASSIA

Borgo Santo
Spirito 1–2–3
Vatican ②
+39 06 6835 2449
aslroma1.it/polo-
museale/complesso-
monumentale-santo-
spirito-in-sassia

What was founded as a hub for 8th-century Saxon pilgrims became one of the most sophisticated hospitals of the era. Its sprawling Sistine Ward surrounds an ornate marble altar by Palladio, his only work in Rome. The courtyard and library are also worth visiting. Viewable by guided tour only, on Mondays at 10 am and 3.30 pm.

305 ANATOMY THEATRE OF SAN GALLICANO HOSPITAL

Via di San
Gallicano 25-A
Trastevere and
Gianicolo ⑦
+39 06 5855 8201-2
inmp.it

Peeking inside Rome hospitals tends to unlock hidden treasures. In San Gallicano, it's an anatomy theatre, commissioned in 1826 by Pope Leo XII. A white slab of marble in the floor marks where the dissecting table was. The room, which is ringed by ornate reliefs of medical allegories, is now a management office. Open Saturdays, 10 am to 4 pm.

301 TEMPLE OF AESCULAPIUS

5
UNDERGROUND
sites you should see

---

306 BARBERINI MITHRAEUM
AT: PALAZZO BARBERINI
Via delle Quattro
Fontane 13
Trident ④
+39 06 3996 7702
coopculture.it

This sanctuary to the sun god Mithras stands out for its colourful 3rd-century illustrations telling the story of the Persian deity, from Mithras slaying a bull, to astrological symbols, to a chronology of his life illustrated along ten paintings. Open the 2nd and 4th Saturday of every month at 10 am, reservation required.

307 VIA LIVENZA HYPOGEUM
Via Livenza 4
Centre North ⑨
+39 06 0608

At the heart of the Salario necropolis lies this lavishly frescoed underground temple. But to what? Its rectangular bath with elaborate plumbing has led some to suspect it was a Christian baptismal hall. Others speculate it was part of a secret water cult, or simply a nymphaeum. Visits on request only.

308 INSULA OF SAN PAOLO ALLA REGOLA

Via di San Paolo alla Regola 16
Centre West ③
+39 06 0608

A layer cake of Roman architecture, stretching four storeys high, two of which are now below street level. The oldest, lower levels were originally a warehouse linked to trade off the Tiber during the reign of Domitian. Two residential storeys were added in the 4th century, then a tower in the 12th. Open daily 9 am to 9 pm by appointment.

309 SANTA PRISCA MITHRAEUM

Via di Santa Prisca 8
Testaccio and Aventino ⑧
+39 06 3996 7702
coopculture.it

Located under the Church of Santa Prisca, the rectangular sanctuary has a barrel-vault with a speleum, a cave representing where the god was born. Inside is a stucco depicting Saturn lying down. The frescoed walls depict the seven initiation phases of Mithraism. Open the 2nd and 4th Saturday of every month at 10 am, reservation required.

310 BASILICA DI SAN CRISOGONO

Piazza Sidney Sonnino 44
Trastevere and Gianicolo ⑦
+39 06 581 0076

A staircase in the sacristy leads down to several layers of sarcophagi and structures predating the present church. The earliest have led some to speculate it was once a secret house church. Little has been done to make the underground area safer or more appealing to tourists, giving the experience an Indiana Jones quality.

5 places from
WWII HISTORY

311 MUSEO STORICO DELLA LIBERAZIONE

Via Tasso 145
Centre East ⑥
+39 06 700 3866
museoliberazione.it/en

The Historical Museum of the Liberation is a moving museum built inside the former headquarters of the German SS. Little has changed inside the nondescript apartment building, including the cell walls where resistance prisoners scrawled their names or notes to their mothers, when they weren't being interrogated, tortured, or killed. Free admission, closed on Monday.

312 MAUSOLEUM OF THE ARDEATINE QUARRIES

Via Ardeatina 174
South Rome ⑭
+39 06 513 6742
mausoleofosse
ardeatine.it

On March 24, 1944, German soldiers executed 335 prisoners at this quarry in retaliation for an Italian resistance bomb attack that killed 33 German soldiers. 'Ten Italians for every German', was the order given. A tunnel at the monument leads to the massacre site, which holds a State commemoration each anniversary.

312 MAUSOLEUM OF THE ARDEATINE QUARRIES

313 PARTISAN ATTACK IN VIA RASELLA

Via Rasella 141
Trident ④

During the Nazi occupation of Rome, on March 23, 1944, a rubbish bin containing 40 pounds of TNT exploded in front of this still-pockmarked building, killing 33 marching German soldiers. The culprits were Italian resistance fighters. The Germans responded by executing 335 prisoners at random.

314 MUSSOLINI'S BALCONY

AT: PALAZZO VENEZIA
Piazza Venezia
Colosseum and
San Giovanni ⑤
+39 06 6999 4211
vive.beniculturali.it/
it/palazzo-venezia

You've seen the historical footage: Il Duce looming over Piazza Venezia, denouncing the Allied Powers while pounding his fist and raising his chin. Throughout the 1930s, the fascist dictator's office was located in the Sala del Mappamondo in the Palazzo Venezia, with a balcony that overlooked the square. After World War II, the balcony was sealed off in disgrace.

315 AIR RAID SIREN

Piazza della Bocca
della Verità 16
Testaccio and
Aventino ⑧

There were about 60 air raid sirens on top of Rome's roofs during World War II. Many of them were removed over time, but there are still 10 in place. They were produced by the company La Sonora, which still exists, and were activated with an electric wire system in case of an imminent attack. This one sticks out above the roof of the Fondazione Teatro dell'Opera di Roma and is best seen from the Circus Maximus.

5

NON-CATHOLIC

sites

---

316 CHIESA DI SANTA CATERINA MARTIRE

Via del Lago
Terrione 77–79
Trastevere and
Gianicolo ⑦

In 2004, this Russian Orthodox church was completed, the first in Rome since the East-West Schism in 1054. Painters from Russia were brought in to decorate the interior. That and the onion-shaped dome make the church distinctly Eastern in style, while just a short walk from the Vatican.

317 GRANDE MOSCHEA

Viale della
Moschea 85
Centre North ⑨
+39 06 808 2258

It's the biggest mosque in Europe. Rome hardly has the biggest Muslim population in Europe, but this is, after all, a global religious centre. Even the Mormons have their biggest European temple in the Eternal City. Pope John Paul II gave his discreet approval but his blessing came with one caveat: the minaret had to be one metre lower than the cupola of St. Peter's.

318 HUA YI SI

Via dell'Omo 142
East Rome ⑬
+39 06 2242 8876

Europe's largest Buddhist temple, which caters primarily to Rome's burgeoning Chinese community. Opened in 2013, it's built in the traditional form of a pagoda, standing out among the industrial buildings in this area. It also contains a full-service vegetarian restaurant for up to 200 diners.

319 ANCIENT SYNAGOGUE

Vicolo dell'Atleta 14
Trastevere and
Gianicolo ⑦

Long before there was the Ghetto, Rome's first Jewish community was concentrated on this side of the Tiber. Traces of the medieval synagogue, which burned down in 1268, are visible in the beautiful arcaded loggia down this alley too narrow for cars. Its central column still bears Hebrew writing.

320 JEWISH CEMETERY UNDER THE MUNICIPAL ROSE GARDEN

Via di Valle Murcia 6
Testaccio and
Aventino ⑧
+39 06 574 6810

Few know that beneath this rose garden lie the remains of thousands of Jews. Pope Innocent X established it in 1645 as a Jewish burial ground. In the 1930s, Fascist authorities built a park over it, and failed to transport all the bodies. In the 1950s it was redesigned, with Ten Commandments placed at each entrance, and its paths forming a Menorah.

COMPLESSO DEL FORO ITALICO

65 PLACES TO ENJOY CULTURE

5 **CONTEMPORARY ART** *galleries* —————— 172

5 **NON-PROFIT** *art galleries* —————— 174

5 *museums you can see* **FOR FREE** —————— 176

5 **FRESCOES** *not to miss* —————— 179

5 **MOSAICS** *you should see* —————— 181

The 5 most charming **ARTISTS' HOUSES** —————— 184

5 *extraordinary* **SCULPTURES** —————— 186

5 *public* **ART INSTALLATIONS** —————— 189

5 *cool* **STREET ART** *pieces* —————— 191

5 *spots for* **MOVIE LOVERS** —————— 194

5 *places to enjoy* **LIVE MUSIC** —————— 196

The 5 best **INTERNATIONAL MOVIE THEATRES** —————— 198

5 **FESTIVALS** *to check out* —————— 200

5
CONTEMPORARY ART
galleries

---

321 **INDIPENDENZA**
Via dei Mille 6
Centre East ⑥
+39 06 4470 3249
indipendenzaroma.com

The exhibition space alone is worth a detour: it's an apartment on the 4th floor of a 20th-century building, featuring precious flooring and frescoed ceilings, turned into a gallery. Three times a year, it showcases works by international contemporary artists, such as Mélanie Matranga and Clément Rodzielski.

322 **VON BUREN CONTEMPORARY**
Via Giulia 13
Centre West ③
+39 335 163 3518
vonburen contemporary.com

This gallery specialises in 'accessible art', i.e. art that doesn't break the bank, with a focus on emerging talent. Featuring artists from Rome and abroad, Von Buren hosts a lively series of new exhibits and events in one of the city's most historic neighbourhoods.

323 **GALLERIA LORCAN O'NEILL ROMA**
Vicolo de' Catinari 3
Centre West ③
+39 06 6889 2980
lorcanoneill.com

Opened in 2003, Galleria Lorcan O'Neill works with top international artists like Martin Creed, Richard Long, Kiki Smith, Jeff Wall and Rachel Whiteread - most of whom have exhibited in Italy for the first time at the gallery. They also show influential Italian artists such as Enrico Castellani and Emilio Prini.

324 **NOMAS FOUNDATION**
Viale Somalia 33
Centre North ⑨
+39 06 8639 8381
nomasfoundation.com

An impressive collection of contemporary art superstars, such as Jannis Kounellis, Marina Abramović, and Joseph Beuys, as well as lesser-known artists. Founded in 2008, the foundation hosts exhibits, seminars, and residencies for artists, curators and critics. Open Tuesday to Friday, from 2.30 to 7 pm.

325 **WUNDERKAMMERN**
Via Gabrio
Serbelloni 124
East Rome ⑫
+39 06 4543 5662
wunderkammern.net

Opened in 2008, the gallery represents emerging, mid-career and established artists, with an emphasis on relational art and public art, such as street artist Invader, whose work can be found on many Rome buildings. Visits by appointment only.

322 VON BUREN CONTEMPORARY

5

NON-PROFIT

art galleries

---

326 **FONDAZIONE PASTIFICIO CERERE**
Via degli Ausoni 7
Centre East ⑥
+39 06 4542 2960
pastificiocerere.it

Built as an industrial pasta factory in 1905 (hence the name), the enormous space today plays host to an array of solo and group exhibitions of painting, sculpture, video, photography and installations, as well as artist studios, classrooms, and a full-service bar and restaurant.

326 FONDAZIONE PASTIFICIO CERERE

327 SALA 1

Piazza di Porta
San Giovanni 10
Centre East ⑥
+39 06 700 8691
salauno.com

Once a church, the art gallery took
shape in 1967, as it was transformed by
the friar and sculptor Tito Amodei into
a sanctuary for contemporary art. Located
in the complex of the Pontifical Sanctuary
of the Scala Santa in San Giovanni, this
experimental research centre also hosts
performances and music concerts.

328 FONDAZIONE GIULIANI

Via Gustavo Bianchi 1
Testaccio and
Aventino ⑧
+39 06 5730 1091
fondazionegiuliani.org

Fondazione Giuliani features 400 works
from the private collection of owner
Giovanni Giuliani, as well as a beautiful
rose-filled courtyard. A convenient stop
for those planning a contemporary art day
around the nearby Mattatoio art museum.

329 ALBUMARTE

Via Flaminia 122
Centre North ⑨
+39 06 2440 2941
albumarte.org

Video art, photography, sculpture,
installations, sound art, performances,
but also residencies and concerts: this
gallery's program is versatile and tends
to focus on the work of young artists and
curators, both Italian and international,
thanks to collaborations with cultural
institutions and academies.

330 BASEMENT ROMA

Via Nicola Ricciotti 4
Vatican ②
+39 06 9435 8667
basementroma.com

This exhibitions space is run by a contemporary art magazine, called CURA, in the
basement of their editorial office. Its goal
is to promote new international talents,
as they showcase the work of artists who
have never had a show in Rome or Italy
before. It also offers a residency program
for artists, writers and publishers.

5 museums you can see
FOR FREE

---

331 MUSEO DI SCULTURA ANTICA GIOVANNI BARRACCO

Corso Vittorio Emanuele II 166-A Centre West ③
+39 06 0608
museobarracco.it

This beautiful building from the 15th century hosts the collection of Giovanni Barracco, donated to Rome in 1902. It consists of 380 pieces from the Near East (mostly Egypt, Cyprus, and Greece). In the 1970s, a 4th-century Roman structure was found underneath and some of the recovered frescoes are on display on the ground floor.

331 MUSEO DI SCULTURA ANTICA GIOVANNI BARRACCO

332 VILLA DI MASSENZIO

Via Appia Antica 153
South Rome ⑭
+39 06 0608
villadimassenzio.it

Built in the second century AD, this rustic villa once belonged to Emperor Maxentius – the same emperor whose dead body was decapitated after his defeat by Constantine at the Milvian Bridge. Today his villa stands out in rustic decay off the Appian Way amid a bucolic backdrop of the Alban Hills. As a nice bonus, the Villa complex contains the remains of a circus (racetrack for horse carriages). This circus is second in size only to the Circo Massimo, but it is better preserved.

332 VILLA DI MASSENZIO

333 MUSEO CARLO BILOTTI

**Viale Fiorello
La Guardia 6
Centre North** ⑨
+39 06 0608
museocarlobilotti.it

Immersed in the park of Villa Borghese, the Orangerie presents the private collection of the entrepreneur Carlo Bilotti, who donated it to the city. It comprises 23 pieces of contemporary art, the most prominent ones by Giorgio de Chirico (one of his sculptures is installed outside the museum). Other artists featured are Andy Warhol, Larry Rivers, Gino Severini, and Giacomo Manzù.

334 MUSEO PIETRO CANONICA

**Viale Pietro
Canonica 2
Centre North** ⑨
+39 06 884 2279
museocanonica.it

Another small but precious find in the Villa Borghese park! This fortress-like building houses the workshop and private apartment of Pietro Canonica, an Italian sculptor who moved in this location in 1927. Walking through the two floors, you can see both his completed and unfinished works, like marbles, bronzes, sketches, studies, models and replicas, which will help you better understand his creative process.

335 MUSEO NAPOLEONICO

**Piazza di Ponte
Umberto I 1
Centre West** ③
+39 06 0608
museonapoleonico.it

A private collection – conceived as an account of the family history and its ties with the city of Rome – of Napoleonic memorabilia, assembled by count Giuseppe Primoli, son of Count Pietro Primoli and Princess Carlotta Bonaparte. It narrates the fortunes of the man rather than the emperor and shows daily life moments of the household.

5
FRESCOES
not to miss

---

336 PAINTED LOGGIA OF PALAZZO ALTEMPS

AT: MUSEO NAZIONALE ROMANO – PALAZZO ALTEMPS

Piazza di Sant'Apollinare 46 Centre West ③

+39 06 684 851

museonazionale romano.beniculturali. it/en/palazzo-altemps

A garden of meticulously painted trompe-l'oeil pergola, flowers and birds, the north loggia alone is worth the admission fee to Palazzo Altemps. Frescos of ornate floral themes were a novelty in urban Rome when the loggia was painted in the late 16th century. Don't miss the painted fountain on the east wall.

337 BASILICA DI SANTO STEFANO ROTONDO AL CELIO

Via Santo Stefano Rotondo 7 Colosseum and San Giovanni ⑤

+39 06 421 199

cgu.it/it/santo-stefano-rotondo

The unassuming façade and its cruciform plan disguise a unique circular interior, covered in gory frescoes, and mosaics. The 34 images from the 16th century portray scenes of martyrdom by Pomarancio and others. Built in the 4th century, the church also preserves a 2nd-century mithraeum and a marble throne of Saint Gregory. It's the Hungarian National church in Rome.

338 PALAZZO PAMPHILJ

Piazza Navona 14
Centre West ③
+39 06 839 8285

Not to be mistaken with Palazzo Doria Pamphilj, this stately palace in Piazza Navona houses the Brazilian embassy, which restored the building's Renaissance frescoes of the life of Aeneas, the mythical founder of Rome whom the Pamphilj dynasty claims as an ancestor. Public visits take place on select days at 3.30 pm, by making reservations online at: *ambasciatadelbrasile.it/palacio/ visita_guidata.asp.*

339 CASINO MASSIMO LANCELLOTTI

Via Matteo Boiardo 16
Centre East ⑥
+39 06 7049 5651

Rooms are frescoed with 18th-century depictions of Italian classical literature, such as Ariosto's *Orlando Furioso* and Dante's *Divine Comedy.* The cycle is considered a masterpiece of the Nazarene movement of German Romantic artists. The Mannerist palazzo dates back to the late 17th century, and today hosts a delegation of Franciscan missionaries to the Holy Land.

340 GONFALONE ORATORY

Via del Gonfalone 32-A
Centre West ③
+39 06 687 5952
oratoriogonfalone.eu

Nicknamed the Sistine Chapel of Mannerism, the Gonfalone Oratory stands out for its elaborate wall frescoes depicting scenes of the Passion. Owing to its wooden ceiling and remarkable acoustics, the oratory hosts regular liturgical concerts, which are the best chance to peek inside the space which is otherwise closed to the public. Visit the website for performance schedules, or call for special appointments.

5

MOSAICS

you should see

---

341 OSTIENSE TRAIN STATION
Piazzale dei Partigiani
Testaccio and Aventino ⑧

Built in honour of Hitler's ensuing visit to Rome in 1938, the Ostiense Train Station is quintessentially Fascist in design, complete with a foreboding travertine façade. Upon entering the columned portico, look down at the floor mosaic of black and white tiles depicting sea creatures and ancient heroes raising their arm in the Roman salute that was adopted by Mussolini.

342 DOMUS OF PORTA MARINA
AT: MUSEO NAZIONALE DELL'ALTO MEDIOEVO
Viale Lincoln 3
South Rome ⑭
+39 06 549 521
museocivilta.cultura. gov.it/alto-medioevo

A shining example of *opus sectile,* the ancient Roman technique of marble inlay, the compositions vividly portray the patricians as well as lions and tigers devouring their prey. The Domus was painstakingly reconstructed here from the collapsed ruins in Ostia. Chronically underappreciated, the museum will love you for coming.

342 MUSEO NAZIONALE DELL'ALTO MEDIOEVO

345 COMPLESSO DEL FORO ITALICO

343 BASILICA DI SANTA PUDENZIANA

Via Urbana 160
Trident ④
+39 06 481 4622
stpudenziana.org

Among the oldest Christian mosaics in Rome inside Rome's oldest church, the heavily restored composition inside the apse is doubly noteworthy for its depiction of Christ in human form. It was much more common to portray him as a lamb or the good shepherd when the mosaic was made, around the year 400.

344 BASILICA DI SANTA PRASSEDE

Via di Santa Prassede 9
Colosseum and San Giovanni ⑤
+39 06 488 2456

The church to duck into when everyone else is crowding inside the nearby Santa Maria Maggiore. Come for the dazzling gilded mosaics in and around the apse, which seem more fitting for Ravenna than for Rome. Stay for the peace and tranquillity right off one of the city's noisiest neighbourhoods.

345 COMPLESSO DEL FORO ITALICO

Piazza Lauro De Bosis
Aurelio ①
+39 06 0608

Foro Italico was originally called Foro Mussolini, which explains its imposing architecture, idealised (read: homoerotic) statues, and Fascist mosaics celebrating military victories and sporting events, while never missing an opportunity to splash a Fascist slogan or Mussolini's name, initials, and nickname: Duce.

The 5 most charming
ARTISTS' HOUSES

---

346 GIORGIO DE CHIRICO HOME MUSEUM

Piazza di Spagna 31
Trident ④
+39 06 679 6546
fondazionede
chirico.org/casa-museo

Best known for his metaphysical style that inspired surrealism, de Chirico would embrace neo-classical and baroque themes later in his career. So it's fitting that the Greek-born Italian artist would choose to live in the heart of Rome when he was 60. The space faithfully preserves the living space and studio, keeping it alive with rotating exhibitions.

347 CASA BALLA

Via Oslavia 39-B
Vatican ②
maxxi.art/events/
casa-balla

In 30 years' time, artist Giacomo Balla, one of the frontrunners of early-20th-century Italian avant-garde Futurism, transformed his family home into a work of art. He lived here from 1929 until his death in 1958 and nothing was spared from his creative and experimental touch, from walls to furniture, utensils, objects, and clothes.

348 LUIGI PIRANDELLO'S STUDIO

Via Antonio
Bosio 13-B
Centre East ⑥
+39 06 4429 1853
*studiodiluigi
pirandello.it*

The home of the Nobel Prize-winning writer until his death in 1936. Located on the top floor of a villa, it includes an institute and library dedicated to his poems, novels and plays that would give birth to the Theatre of the Absurd. Personal items, such as family pictures and his typewriter, are on display. Open Monday to Friday by appointment.

349 CASA MUSEO ALBERTO MORAVIA

Lungotevere
della Vittoria 1
Vatican ②
+39 06 320 3698
casaalbertomoravia.it

Simple and modern furniture characterise the home of Moravia, one of Italy's great existentialist authors. His original bookshelves still crowd against the walls, along with paintings and work on paper by friends such as Renato Guttuso, who painted Moravia's portrait. Visits by appointment, every second Saturday of the month.

350 KEATS-SHELLEY HOUSE

Piazza di Spagna 26
Trident ④
+39 06 678 4235
ksh.roma.it

For the Romantic spirits who agree that "a thing of beauty is a joy forever" and "the soul's joy lies in doing", this memorial house to British bad boys of poetry John Keats and Percy Bysshe Shelley provides a corner of peaceful beauty and joy amid the hustle and bustle of the Spanish Steps.

5 extraordinary
SCULPTURES

---

351 **BERNINI'S TWO ANGELS**
AT: BASILICA DI SANT'
ANDREA DELLE FRATTE
**Via di Sant'Andrea
delle Fratte 1**
Trident ④
+39 06 679 3191

Perhaps you've already seen angels identical to these on the Castel Sant'Angelo Bridge. In fact, those are the copies. Pope Clement IX deemed Bernini's late-17th-century originals too precious to be exposed to the elements. Today they're at the sides of the presbytery.

352 **ECSTASY OF BLESSED LUDOVICA ALBERTONI BY BERNINI**
AT: CHIESA DI
SAN FRANCESCO
D'ASISISI A RIPA
**Piazza di San
Francesco d'Assisi 88**
**Trastevere and
Gianicolo** ⑦
+39 06 581 9020

Bernini said he was trying to portray the ecstasy of communing with God. But for centuries, naughty observers have perceived an ecstasy of the carnal nature in the sculpture of Ludovica Albertoni, much as they have in Bernini's more famous *Ecstasy of Saint Teresa* (inside Rome's Santa Maria della Vittoria). You decide.

353 SARCOPHAGUS OF THE SPOUSES

AT: MUSEO NAZIONALE
ETRUSCO DI VILLA GIULIA

**Piazzale di Villa
Giulia 9**

Centre North ⑨

+39 06 322 6571

museoetru.it

A masterpiece from the Etruscan period, which very few bother to visit in this museum just outside the main tourist habitat. Dating back to the 6th century BC, the sarcophagus depicts a couple reclining merrily at a banquet in the afterlife. Excavated in Cerveteri in the 19th-century, it has beguiled art historians ever since.

354 BOXER AT REST

AT: MUSEO
NAZIONALE ROMANO –
PALAZZO MASSIMO

Largo Villa Peretti 2

**Colosseum and
San Giovanni** ⑤

*museonazionale
romano.beniculturali.it*

A stunning example of bronze sculpture to survive Hellenism without being melted down, perhaps for its exceptional beauty and realism: this is not the triumphant victor, but the battered brute, with swollen cheeks, crooked nose, and open wounds. A must-see.

354 **BOXER AT REST**

355 **SCULPTURES OF CHARITY AND TRUTH**
AT: CAPPELLA DA SYLVA,
SAINT ISIDORE'S COLLEGE
Via degli Artisti 41
Trident ④
+39 06 488 5359
stisidoresrome.org

During restoration work at the chapel in 2002, a discovery was made: the bronze drapery that clothed *Truth* and *Charity* was not part of Bernini's design, but was added by sheepish priests in the 19th century. Provocatively, Bernini had sculpted them bare-breasted. The 'brassieres' have since been removed. Visits by appointment.

352 ECSTASY OF BLESSED LUDOVICA ALBERTONI

5 public
ART INSTALLATIONS

356 **STOLPERSTEINE**
Via Arenula 29
Centre West ③
stolpersteine.eu

Just one of thousands of brass cobblestones embedded in the road throughout the city, each bearing the name and life dates of a resident who was killed or persecuted by the Nazis. Begun in 1992 by German artist Gunter Demnig, the project is ongoing, with cobbles in 22 European countries.

357 **SPACE INVADER**
Via del Pigneto,
at the crossroads
with Via L'Aquila
Centre East ⑥
space-invaders.com/
world/rome

In the summer of 2010, Romans awoke one morning to find their city had been blanketed with crude, pixelated monsters from 1980s videogames. They were installed by renowned street artist Invader. Few survive, but this is one of them, affixed on the mustard-yellow building leading into the pedestrian area.

358 **'TRIUMPHS**
AND LAMENTS'
William Kentridge's
Piazza Tevere
(betw Ponte Sisto
and Ponte Mazzini)
Centre West ③

The cement banks of the Tiber River have long been regarded as a no-man's land, covered in a layer of soot and graffiti. In 2016, artist William Kentridge erased from that patina a 500-metre-long frieze, composed of over 80 figures, up to 9-metres high, from the ancient and contemporary history of Rome.

359 VILLA GLORI
Piazzale del Parco della Rimembranza Centre North ⑨
sovraintendenza roma.it

The park conceals a sculpture garden of contemporary art, so expect large-scale abstracts as opposed to the Rodins you find in many major European cities. Unlike most urban parks in Rome, Villa Glori is not a former aristocratic estate, but an old hunting ground, hence the modest lodge as opposed to a grand villa at its core.

360 EX MIRA LANZA MUSEUM / M.A.G.R.
Via Amedeo Avogadro 85 Trastevere and Gianicolo ⑦
999contemporary.com/ exmiralanza

An abandoned soap factory converted into a mesmerising 'museum' by French street artist Seth. It's managed by a homeless family that squats on the premises and gives tours, living off proceeds of the catalogs. Admission is free, but getting in is tricky: look for a gap in the chain-link fence at the above address.

359 VILLA GLORI

5 cool
STREET ART
pieces

361 **I VOLTI DI BLU**
AT: EX CASERMA
DELL'AERONAUTICA
**Via del Porto
Fluviale 2
South Rome** ⑭
blublu.org

The windows of this rainbow-coloured building have become the eyes of psychedelic lifeforms. They're the creation of Italian street artist Blu, who spent two years living with the 450 squatters who occupy this former air force barracks while he painted it, calling it 'one of the best experiences' of his life.

362 **SANBA**
**Via Argentina
Altobelli 32
Tiburtino** ⑪
onthewalls.it

Put a bird on it. Lots of them. That's what artists Agostino Iacurci, Liqen and Hitnes did to Sanba, short for this area of the San Basilio neighbourhood. Surrounding a playground, the murals also include giant cats, frogs, and flowers from what looks like Lewis Carroll's idea of a rainforest. Start your walk in Via Argentina Altobelli and explore this colourful neighbourhood from there.

361 I VOLTI DI BLU

363 WALL OF FAME
Via dei Magazzini
Generali
South Rome ⑭

A who's who of the personalities that influenced artist JB Rock, painted in alphabetical order, from vDante Alighieri to Zorro (a self-portrait of the artist). Extending nearly 60 metres, the parade of black-and-white faces on a red background includes Barack Obama, Pope John Paul II, Ray Charles, Malcolm X, and Quentin Tarantino.

364 MUSEO MAAM
Via Prenestina 913
East Rome ⑫

MAAM, an acronym that stands for Museum of the Other and the Elsewhere Metropoliz, is set inside a squat in the Rome outskirts. Its residents are some of the artists. Through word of mouth, they've invited universities, galleries, independent curators, and random people to take part since 2012. Open Saturdays.

365 STRANIERA
Viale dell'Acquedotto
Alessandrino
East Rome ⑬

The work by Moscow-based Alexey Luka translates to '(Female) Foreigner'. In a style akin to Picasso's cubism, distorted shapes converge to form a woman's face, encompassing the entire side of this residential building. The colour scheme is in harmony with the surrounding cityscape.

5 spots for
MOVIE LOVERS

---

366 MIAC

Via Tuscolana 1055
East Rome ⑫
+39 06 7229 3269
museomiac.it

An interactive and immersive multimedia museum opened in 2019 that is devoted to the history of the motion picture, from the origins of cinema to the advent of television and digital technologies. Twelve rooms filled with archival documents and hundreds of historic clips, photos and interviews.

367 'WE HAVE A POPE'

AT: CHIESA DI
SANTA DOROTEA
Via di Santa
Dorotea 23
Trastevere and
Gianicolo ⑦
+39 06 580 6205

In Nanni Moretti's acclaimed 2011 film *We Have a Pope* (*Habemus Papam*), a cardinal is reluctantly elected pontiff, suffers a panic attack, and flees the Vatican. While on the run, he ducks into the Church of Santa Dorotea and attends Mass. Around the corner in Piazza Trilussa, he stops at a newsstand to read the headlines about himself.

368 'SPECTRE, 007'

AT: MUSEO DELLA
CIVILTÀ ROMANA
Piazza G. Agnelli 10
South Rome ⑭
museociviltaromana.it

In 2015, Rome reclaimed its old nickname, 'Hollywood on the Tiber', with big-budget films lured by fat tax breaks. One such film was *Spectre*, which saw James Bond (Daniel Craig) racing cars down the banks of the Tiber, and appearing outside this museum.

369 **'ROME, OPEN CITY'**
  Via Montecuccoli 17
  Centre East ⑥

Roberto Rossellini's 1945 neo-realist landmark film was shot in Rome's war-torn streets. One of them was Via Montecuccoli, in the Pigneto neighbourhood. In the final scene, Anna Magnani's character Pina is shot dead hereby the Germans as they take her husband prisoner. A plaque marks the spot.

370 **'MAMMA ROMA'**
  AT: BASILICA DI
  SAN GIOVANNI BOSCO
  Viale dei Salesiani 9
  East Rome ⑫

Pasolini's *Mamma Roma* was a scandal in its day. When it premiered in Rome, Pasolini was attacked by Fascists for its 'indecent' language and content – prostitutes and thieves. In the final scene, Anna Magnani's character Mamma Roma nearly hurls herself from the window, then catches a glance at this basilica and reconsiders.

368 'SPECTRE, 007'

5 places to enjoy
LIVE MUSIC

---

371 ELLINGTON CLUB
Via Anassimandro 15
East Rome ⑫
+39 392 111 0282
ellingtonclubroma.com

Featuring burlesque, live music, stand-up comedy, dinner, brunch and cocktails, Ellington Club takes you back to the days of cancan and Toulouse-Lautrec. Tucked away in Rome's edgy Pigneto neighbourhood, this place is frequented by international celebrities like Bill Murray and Wes Anderson.

372 LANIFICIO
Via di Pietralata 159
Tiburtino ⑪
+39 06 4178 0081
lanificio.com

Lanificio means 'wool mill', an homage to previous tenants. Today they're churning out quality live music, DJ sets and modern art exhibits. This eclectic space also offers a full-service restaurant with nouvelle cuisine. Check out the rooftop garden overlooking the Aniene River.

373 CASA DEL JAZZ
Viale di Porta
Ardeatina 55
Testaccio and
Aventino ⑧
+39 06 8024 1281
casajazz.it

If you're lucky, you may catch Paolo Fresu, Enrico Rava, or any number of Italy's jazz stars performing in what is Rome's premiere jazz concert hall. Nestled in a leafy park, what was once a mobster's villa today has a 150-seat performance space, perfect acoustics, and a charming cafe.

374 MARMO

Piazzale del Verano 71
Centre East ⑥
+39 06 4559 5904

Founded in 2013 when three friends decided to turn an old marble tombstone factory into a night spot. Located across the historic Verano cemetery, it's also in the hip San Lorenzo neighbourhood, offering good cocktails, a great patio, and live music ranging from rock and hip-hop to DJ sets.

375 NUOVO CINEMA PALAZZO

Piazza dei Sanniti 9-A
Centre East ⑥
nuovocinemapalazzo.it

This former movie theatre was about to become a casino when locals organised to block the effort and opened this community centre instead. Live, local music with a subversive bent is the norm. It also offers breakdancing courses, plays, and workshops on child development.

The 5 best

INTERNATIONAL MOVIE THEATRES

---

376 CINEMA NUOVO SACHER

Largo Ascianghi 1
Trastevere and
Gianicolo ⑦
+39 06 581 8116
sacherfilm.eu

Once a clubhouse for public-sector employees in the 1930s, this single-screen art-house movie theatre is the brainchild of iconic filmmaker Nanni Moretti. In addition to the 362-seat single-screen indoor theatre, you can catch outdoor projections in the adjacent amphitheatre in the summer. There's also a bar and a cinema-centric bookstore.

377 CASA DEL CINEMA
AT: VILLA BORGHESE PARK

Largo Marcello
Mastroianni 1
Centre North ⑨
+39 06 423 601
casadelcinema.it

A movie theatre set against the leafy backdrop of the Villa Borghese park. The line-up is dedicated to quality films in all genres, including historical and documentary. It includes an exhibition space – past themes have included the films of Barbra Streisand, Pier Paolo Pasolini, and the cinema of Sicily. It also has a lovely cafe offering excellent shade in the park.

378 CINEMA NUOVO OLIMPIA

Via in Lucina 16
Trident ④
+39 06 8880 1283
circuitocinema.com

A hub among Rome's English-speaking expat community, offering a rich selection of award-winning films from Hollywood to Europe and beyond in their original language. Its two screening rooms occasionally put on special events with filmmakers and actors. Bring your patience to the box office – customer service is notoriously low.

379 CINEMA DEI PICCOLI

AT: VILLA BORGHESE PARK
Viale della Pineta 15
Centre North ⑨
+39 06 855 3485
cinemadeipiccoli.com

In 2005 Cinema dei PIccoli entered the Guinness World Records list for being the smallest movie theatre in the world: to this day, it only has 63 (unnumbered) seats! While it mainly shows cartoons and movies dedicated to a young audience, they also offer foreign films in the original language for grown-ups at night. Check website for listings.

380 MULTISALA BARBERINI

Piazza Barberini 24–26
Trident ④
+39 06 4201 0392
barberini.18tickets.it

The biggest of the selection, this movie theatre has five screening rooms, ranging from 90 to 400 seats, right in the city centre. Most screenings are in Italian, however they do project some movies in the original language. Check the program, and look for 'versione originale' or 'lingua inglese', to make sure that that's the case.

5

FESTIVALS

to check out

---

381 IL CINEMA IN PIAZZA
Piazza San Cosimato
Trastevere and
Gianicolo ⑦
ilcinemainpiazza.it

Trastevere's least touristy square becomes an open-air movie theatre for two months in summer (check the website for dates and screenings). It's free, and without reservations, so come early to claim a spot. The concept has also spread to the Tor Sapienza and Monte Ciocci neighbourhoods, if you want to trailblaze. In addition to film screenings, there are also talks with directors, actors, and screenwriters, as well as retrospectives.

382 OPEN HOUSE ROMA
openhouseroma.org

A free, annual weekend event in which hundreds of otherwise private buildings open their doors to the public. Sites range from Renaissance homes to hyper-modern ateliers, and even sites under construction, with guided tours available. The event usually takes place in the spring. Check the site for details.

383 GIORNATE FAI DI PRIMAVERA
giornatefai.it

Modeled after Britain's National Trust, FAI is the country's primary conservation organisation. Every spring they offer a weekend of events and guided tours in protected areas around the country. In Rome they tend to include recently restored sites such as the Domus Aurea. Check the site for the schedule.

384 ROMAEUROPA FESTIVAL
VARIOUS LOCATIONS, CHECK WEBSITE FOR PROGRAMME
romaeuropa.net

One of the most successful festivals in Lazio (and Italy) for contemporary dance, theatre and music, from September until the end of November. Each year, a new theme brings dozens of acclaimed international and national artists along with emerging performers to Rome. Events take place in several locations across town, so ticket prices vary.

385 ROMA SUMMER FEST
AT: AUDITORIUM PARCO DELLA MUSICA
Viale Pietro de Coubertin 30 Centre North ⑨
+39 06 8024 1281
auditorium.com/ rassegna/roma_ summer_fest_2022- 22590.html

A summer music festival at the eye-catching open-air Auditorium Parco della Musica, designed by starchitect Renzo Piano. Performances feature a mix of rising, established, and fading stars, and have included such high calibres as Elton John, Sting, Björk, Leonard Cohen, Bob Dylan, The National, Paolo Conte, Patti Smith, Arctic Monkeys, Simple Minds, Ringo Starr, Mogwai, Franz Ferdinand, Steven Tyler, and Shaggy.

CANNONBALL IN FRONT OF VILLA MEDICI

30 THINGS TO DO WITH CHILDREN

5 family-friendly RESTAURANTS —————————— 204

5 great SHOPS for kids —————————— 206

5 fun activities for a RAINY DAY —————————— 208

5 amusing OUTDOOR ACTIVITIES ————————— 210

5 ANCIENT GAMES to discover ————————— 212

5 unexpected places to find CANNONBALLS ——— 214

5 family-friendly
RESTAURANTS

386 NUMA AL CIRCO
Viale Aventino 20
Colosseum and
San Giovanni ⑤
+39 06 6442 0669
numaroma.it

A great family-friendly restaurant with outdoor seating in a very touristy area that was surprisingly lacking a good, reliable spot. The menu is varied without being overly complicated, featuring both excellent pastas and pizzas. Should the kids need to blow off some steam, cross the street and let them run a few laps in the Circus Maximus while you order yourself a nice drink or two.

387 CICLOSTAZIONE FRATTINI
Via P. Frattini 136
West Rome ⑬
+39 06 550 3707
ciclostazionefrattini.it

This restaurant has a play area for children with trampolines, a ball pit, a jungle gym, and other activities, with professional entertainers on hand to supervise and put on workshops for different age groups during dinner. The cuisine and atmosphere is nevertheless sophisticated.

388 VIVI BISTROT
AT: VILLA DORIA PAMPHILJ
Via Vitellia 102
Trastevere and
Gianicolo ⑦
+39 06 582 7540
vivibistrot.com

While ViVi Bistrot has several branches in the city, we particularly like their instalment within Rome's biggest public park, Villa Doria Pamphilj. Here kids have plenty of space to run around. The food is very healthy and tasty, all organic, including the fruit and veggie juices. If you prefer to stay in nature, they also offer picnic menus, which come in biodegradable packaging.

389 PIRATI PUB
Via Mario
Menghini 97
South Rome ⑭
+39 06 7834 8579

This pirate-themed pub isn't created around children, but the playful environment makes for a kid-friendly experience, particularly if they're a bit older. In the afternoon, the pub is also a shop for purchasing bottled beer to take away, while during the evening it's a relaxing environment to enjoy a craft beer, watch the football game, or use the free Wi-Fi.

390 CASETTE DI CAMPAGNA
Via di Affogalasino 40
West Rome ⑬
+39 06 6574 3230
casettedicampagna.it

Casette di Campagna is a villa on the edge of the city, with both a restaurant and pizzeria, using high-quality local ingredients. For kids, there's ample outdoor space, with a jungle gym and play park, swings, slides, and seesaws. There's also a small soccer field, and a child-size cafe. Ample parking, by Roman standards.

5 great
S H O P S
for kids

---

391 **RACHELE**
Vicolo del Bollo 7
Centre West ③
+39 329 648 1004

If you're looking for very colourful, handmade kids' clothes, this is the place for you. Rachele's shop is like a rainbow, with stripes, flowers and polka dots everywhere. A great place to buy hats and jackets, dresses and overalls, for boys and girls from age 0 to 12, which are all made in the workshop next to the store.

392 **MAMALÌ**
Via Giovanni
de Calvi 9
Trastevere and
Gianicolo ⑦
+39 06 8308 9243
mamali-giocattoli-educativi.business.site

The owners of Mamalì say they designed the store by constantly kneeling, in order to have a child's perspective. They specialise in educational toys made from wood, but also from other materials such as high-grade plastic. There's also a selection of children's books and candy.

393 **NATINUDI**
Piazza di
San Cosimato 65
Trastevere and
Gianicolo ⑦
+39 06 5834 0014

The name of this baby clothing and children's boutique translates to 'born naked'. It's a delightful place to find unique brands of onesies, coats, tops, pants, and overalls, each cuter than the next. But the prices are not for everyone – a toddler sweater can easily go for 60 euro.

394 TIPI, BAR & STORE

Via Gentile
da Mogliano 168
East Rome ⑫
+39 06 9453 8290

A more comfortable hang-out for kids and parents there could not be. Your child can sip an organic juice while you peruse through the ethically sourced clothing and toys made with non-toxic materials. It's located in the up-and-coming Pigneto neighbourhood, catering to a hip middle class with prices that won't break your budget. The owner, Rossella, is a mom herself and if she doesn't have what you're looking for, she knows who does.

395 LA BOTTEGA DEL SOLDATINO

Via Lago di Lesina 13
Centre North ⑨
+39 06 8621 3452
*labottega
delsoldatino.it*

This family-run workshop specialises in handcrafted lead-cast model tin soldiers. It's been around since 1910, making it the oldest of its kind in Rome, drawing collectors from Italy and abroad. Its models from pre-unification Italy are the most popular, such as the armies of the Papal States and Napoleon.

5 fun activities for a
RAINY DAY

396 MUSEO LEONARDO DA VINCI EXPERIENCE

Via della
Conciliazione 19
Vatican ②
+39 06 683 3316
*leonardodavinci
museo.com*

Here you won't hear museum attendants yell "Do not touch!". Quite the opposite. This is an interactive exhibition showcasing more than 50 full-scale reproductions of Leonardo's machines, so that you can try and figure out, firsthand, how these models work. Good audioguide to boot.

397 EXPLORA

Via Flaminia 80–86
Centre North ⑨
+39 06 361 3776
mdbr.it

Explora is a hands-on museum of the world in miniature, where kids get to feel grown-up. They can pretend to be a farmer, a banker or the ever popular firefighter. There's also a food lab where kids learn to bake cookies. Book ahead.

398 CINEBIMBICITTÀ

AT: CINECITTÀ
Via Tuscolana 1055
East Rome ⑫
+39 06 7229 3269
cinecittasimostra.it

Every Sunday, Rome's famous movie studios, Cinecittà, put on a series of activities for children. For the regular cost of admission, kids get to dress up in movie costumes, learn how to make storyboards and illustrate scenes while learning about the history of cinema. Activities are in Italian, but many don't require speaking.

399 VIGAMUS (VIDEO GAME MUSEUM)

Via Sabotino 4
Vatican ②
+39 06 3751 8325
vigamus.com

Vigamus is a video game museum that starts in the 1950s with *Tennis for Two,* through *Pong* in the 70s, *Pacman* in the 80s, all the way to the virtual reality of today. Many games are available to play for free. Every Monday and Thursday it hosts VR days, where you can experience the Oculus Room.

400 MUSEO DELLA MEMORIA GIOCOSA

Via Marco Vincenzo
Coronelli 26
East Rome ⑬
+39 06 2170 0782
lamemoriagiocosa.it

The Museum of Childhood Memories revolves around the toy collection of an Austrian man who escaped Nazism as a child. As an adult, he continued collecting European, Asian, and American toys. The museum also has a theatre that puts on children's shows. Admission is free. Call ahead for booking.

396 MUSEO LEONARDO DA VINCI EXPERIENCE

5 amusing
OUTDOOR ACTIVITIES

401 BIOPARCO
Viale del Giardino
Zoologico 1
Centre North ⑨
+39 06 360 8211
bioparco.it

Opened in 1911, this zoo hosts over 200 animal species from all five continents, among which are snakes, tigers, giraffes and exotic birds. Over the weekends, they often run fun events to teach kids about animals and the environment. Kids can even feed the elephants!

402 LA FATTORIETTA
Vicolo del
Gelsomino 68
(Via Gregorio VII)
Trastevere and
Gianicolo ⑦
+39 338 291 6918

A hidden gem tucked behind St. Peter's, La Fattorietta is a little farm where children can pick olives and turn them into oil, make bread in a wood-burning stove, milk a goat and make cheese, even pick grapes and make wine. Open 8 am to 5 pm, Monday to Friday. Call ahead to reserve a space.

403 PARCO DEGLI ACQUEDOTTI
Via Lemonia
East Rome ⑫
+39 06 513 5316
parcoacquedotti.it

Not far from the centre of Rome stretch 37 acres of Roman aqueducts through the grassy Roman countryside, an area that originally linked the Alban Hills to ancient Rome. Today it also includes the Felice Aqueduct. It was built by the papacy during the Renaissance and is still used for irrigation.

404 CENTRO HABITAT MEDITERRANEO LIPU OSTIA

Via dell'Idroscalo
Lido di Ostia
+39 379 230 5540
lipu.it/centro-habitat-mediterraneo-ostia

This wetland and wildlife reserve, where the mouth of the Tiber River meets the Tyrrhenian sea, gives one of the most pristine looks at Rome in its natural, unalloyed state. Birdwatching outposts help visitors identify over 200 species, including the rare purple heron. There are also ample trails for hiking.

405 RISERVA NATURALE DELL'INSUGHERATA

Via Paolo Emilio
Castagnola
North Rome ⑩
+39 339 579 3993
insugherata.com

This natural reserve covers more than 1700 acres of different environments, from grazed meadows to forests, wetlands and Roman ruins. Call ahead to ask about nature workshops for children, where they can look at bugs through microscopes on guided hikes beneath pine trees along ancient walls of tufa.

403 PARCO DEGLI ACQUEDOTTI

5

ANCIENT GAMES
to discover

---

406 CARACALLA'S BATHS
Viale delle Terme
di Caracalla 52
Testaccio and
Aventino ⑧
+39 06 3996 7702
coopculture.it

Even the ancient Romans enjoyed board games. Here you can see an example of a *tabula lusoria* etched in the pavement at the edge of the swimming pool adjacent the natatio, so that people could play while immersed in water. This particular game was called *tropa*, or 'hole-game', and consisted in getting walnuts, marbles, or knucklebones into the holes.

407 BASILICA DEI SANTI QUATTRO CORONATI
Via dei Santi
Quattro 20
Colosseum and
San Giovanni ⑤
+39 06 7047 5427
*monacheagostiniane
santiquattrocoronati.it*

As you enter the main cloister to the left of the church, through a tiny door (donation required), you'll soon encounter a strange inscription on a slab of marble between two columns: a series of parallel lines intermixed with signs that look like Roman numbers. Scholars think it may have been a game where players were supposed to spin a top and reach the columns with the highest numbers.

408 DOMITIAN'S STADIUM

Via di Tor
Sanguigna 3
Centre West ③
+39 06 6880 5311
stadiodomiziano.com

It's hard to imagine that this huge area, now covered by Piazza Navona, was once a Circus Agonalis, dedicated to athletic contests. Built under the Emperor Domitian, it hosted such competitions as races, wrestling, boxing, pankration (a brutal form of fighting, with very scarce rules), and the pentathlon, which included discus, javelin, running and wrestling.

409 BASILICA DI SANTA MARIA MAGGIORE

Piazza di Santa
Maria Maggiore 42
Colosseum and
San Giovanni ⑤
+39 06 6988 6800

A palindrome is a word that can be read the same way equally backward and forward. In the archaeological area beneath the basilica, there's an example of such a 'game' that reads 'Roma summus Amor' (Rome supreme Love), and a special 'magic square' that assembles four palindromes, called Sator square, linked to the early Christian tradition.

410 IVORY DOLL OF THE MUMMY OF GROTTAROSSA

AT: MUSEO
NAZIONALE ROMANO –
PALAZZO MASSIMO
Largo Villa Peretti 2
Colosseum and
San Giovanni ⑤
+39 06 480 201
*museonazionale
romano.beniculturali.it*

In 1964, the well preserved mummified body of an eight-year-old girl was found in Grottarossa (North of Rome), dating to the 2nd century. In the sarcophagus, the accompanying funerary kit included precious gold jewellery, and an articulated ivory doll, resembling wood, whose refined features and details attest to the carver's ability.

5 unexpected places to find
CANNONBALLS

---

411 PALAZZO COLONNA

Piazza dei Santissimi
Apostoli 66
Trident ④
+39 06 678 4350
galleriacolonna.it

In 1849, French troops were battling
Garibaldi's soldiers in Rome during the
Risorgimento, when a cannonball came
whizzing through a window of the Palazzo
Colonna. Amazingly, it is still lodged in
the steps of the grand staircase inside,
preserved by the owners as a memento
to Italian unification.

412 VILLA MEDICI

Viale della Trinità
dei Monti 1
Trident ④
+39 06 676 1200
villamedici.it

In front of the entrance of Villa Medici
sits a dramatic fountain made of granite.
In the middle, there's a real cannonball
with water spouting out of its centre. Its
provenance is uncertain, but the story
goes that Queen Christina of Sweden fired
it at the villa in order to wake someone
inside. There are several dents on the door.

413 BASILICA DI SAN BARTOLOMEO ALL'ISOLA TIBERINA

Piazza di San
Bartolomeo
all'Isola 22
Centre West ③
+39 06 687 7973
sanbartolomeo.org

Inside the chapel of the Basilica of Saint Bartholomew on the Tiber Island, you may need to ask a priest to show you 'the miracle'. In 1849, as French troops battled Italians during the Risorgimento, a cannonball flew into the church and was lodged in the wall. It happened during Mass, but no one was hurt.

414 CHIESA DI SAN PIETRO IN MONTORIO

Piazza di San Pietro
in Montorio 2
Trastevere and
Gianicolo ⑦
+39 06 581 3940
sanpietroinmontorio.it

The Gianicolo Hill was a major battleground during Italy's struggle for unification in the mid-19th century. Garibaldi himself was in charge of its defence. One testimony to that is a plaque on the Church of San Pietro in Montorio, hidden around the left side of the façade. There's a French cannonball mounted to its surface.

415 IN THE AURELIAN WALLS

Via Po/Corso d'Italia
Centre North ⑨

Few passers-by seem to notice this souvenir of 1870. On September 20 of that year, Italian troops made their final push to claim Rome for the Kingdom of Italy and expel the last papal loyalists, unleashing a barrage of artillery in the process. This cannonball in the tower above Via Pio is a testimony to that.

CHIOSTRO DEL BRAMANTE ACCOMMODATION

20 PLACES
TO SLEEP

5 hotels with a GREAT VIEW ———————— 218

5 UNUSUAL sleeping accommodations ———— 220

The 5 best BOUTIQUE HOTELS ———————— 222

5 fine DESIGN HOTELS ————————— 224

5 hotels with a
GREAT VIEW

---

416 BIO HOTEL RAPHAËL

Largo Febo 2
Centre West ③
+39 06 682 831
biohotelraphael.com

Just a short walk from the Pantheon in one direction and the Spanish Steps in the other, Bio Hotel Raphaël's rooftop terrace puts you on even footing with the campaniles and cupolas of a phalanx of nearby churches. Not to be missed indoors is the collection of Picasso ceramics and Mayan art.

417 HOTEL PALAZZO MANFREDI

Via Labicana 125
Colosseum and
San Giovanni ⑤
+39 06 7759 1380
palazzomanfredi.com

Built on the grounds where gladiators used to train, this luxury hotel overlooks the Colosseum, the Imperial Forum, the Palatine Hill, and the Caelian Hill. Sharing that view on the terrace is the hotel's Michelin-starred restaurant, Aroma, which specialises in classic Italian dishes.

418 HORTI 14

Via di San Francesco
di Sales 14
Trastevere and
Gianicolo ⑦
+39 06 6880 6289
horti14.com

Each room at this boutique hotel – a former lumberyard – has been decorated by Italian street artist Lucamaleonte with vegetal themes, an artistic homage to the adjacent Botanical Garden, which also serves as a wonderful backdrop to the hotel's rooftop garden-terrace, with an adjacent bar.

419 9HOTEL CESÀRI

Via di Pietra 89-A
Centre West ③
+39 06 674 9701
9-hotel-cesari-rome.it

Truly one of the most privileged vantage points in all of Rome is the Cesàri hotel's rooftop bar. La Terrazza del Cesàri gets its name from its terrace overlooking the Piazza di Pietra and the Temple of Hadrian. From the right angle, you can even spy the tip of the Column of Marcus Aurelius in the adjacent Piazza Colonna.

420 MAMA'S HOME ROME

Piazza Campo
de' Fiori 27
Centre West ③
+39 334 174 6577
mamashomerome.com

Facing the picture-perfect Campo de' Fiori, Mama's Home Rome puts guests eye-to-eye with Giordano Bruno, whose statue occupies the centre of the square. During market hours in the morning, there's no better place to people-watch. Inside, the design of the hotel is a jewel of contemporary and antique fusion.

419 LA TERRAZZA DEL CESÀRI

5

UNUSUAL

sleeping accommodations

421 **THE BEEHIVE**
Via Marghera 8
Centre East ⑥
+39 06 4470 4553
the-beehive.com

Run by an American couple, Linda and Steve, this cosy and charming hybrid between a hostel and a hotel is conveniently located in the Termini area. It's environmentally conscious, with a common lounge area and a garden to relax. Breakfast is not included in the price, but totally worth it. The vegetarian cafe in the basement also hosts vegan aperitifs.

422 **CHIOSTRO DEL BRAMANTE ACCOMMODATION**
Via Arco della Pace 5
Centre West ③
+39 06 6880 9035
chiostrodelbramante.it

A crowning feature of the beautiful church of Santa Maria della Pace is the Bramante cloister. Few people know there are three apartments on the top floor of this complex available to rent. The penthouse is built inside a tower, offering 360-degree views and a massive terrace.

423 IROOMS

several locations
in the city
irooms.it

For the high-tech traveller. Each room comes with an iPad to operate the remote-control features, such as the lights, the 3D TV, and in some rooms, cinema walls that allow you to project the scenery of your choosing. Every room has a different theme, and roughly half of them have a jacuzzi.

424 SOHO HOUSE ROME

Via Cesare de Lollis 14
Centre East ⑥
+39 06 9480 8000
sohohouse.com/
en-us/houses/
soho-house-rome

As the name implies, this hotel was inspired by the eponymous neighbourhood in Manhattan, catering to a well-healed clientele looking to party in style. Located in the bohemian San Lorenzo neighbour-hood, its 10-storey building boasts a rooftop terrace and swimming pool. Each floor has a balcony. The restaurant makes its own pasta, focussing on northern Italian cuisine. On the same floor there's club space for parties and concerts.

425 CASA DI SANTA FRANCESCA ROMANA

Via dei Vascellari 61
Trastevere and
Gianicolo ⑦
+39 06 581 2125
sfromana.it

A former monastery, Casa di Santa Francesca Romana still has an active chapel and reliquary inside where priests read mass. The rooms are still very spartan, but impeccably clean. The courtyard has a fountain and tables for relaxing. Inside there's a large dining hall, with free breakfast.

The 5 best
BOUTIQUE HOTELS

426 ABITART HOTEL
Via Pellegrino
Matteucci 10-20
South Rome ⑭
+39 06 454 3191
abitarthotel.com

Abitart is a keenly designed contemporary hotel accentuated with colourful avant-garde artwork throughout, such as the playful *Bocca delle Bugie* (we'll let you look for that one). The hotel is located just down the street from Eataly, the fine food emporium, in an unassuming neighbourhood with great restaurants and bars.

427 HOTEL SAN ANSELMO
Piazza San Anselmo 2
Testaccio and
Aventino ⑧
+39 06 570 057
aventinohotels.com

Sofia Coppola would probably feel at home in this whimsically elegant hotel, which mixes stucco molding and art deco design with eclectic contemporary artworks. Housed inside a villa on the Aventine Hill, Hotel San Anselmo captures the verdant tranquility unique to the neighbourhood.

428 HOTEL TEATRO PACE
Via del Teatro
Pace 33
Centre West ③
+39 06 687 9075
hotelteatropace.com

Once a cardinal's palace in the 16th century, Hotel Teatro Pace maintains the same baroque ambience, with charming narrow hallways and stone staircases. Its rooms have exquisitely restored parquet floors, complimenting the mahogany furniture.

429 CASACAU

Via in Arcione 94
Trident ④
+39 06 6929 0159
casacau.com

Casacau makes the option of renting an apartment exciting. Each of the six apartments is impeccably designed, and all have a dining space and open kitchen. Guests are provided with fresh groceries for breakfast. Four have a Turkish bath, one sports a sauna. Vintage-cool vibes.

430 THE FIFTEEN KEYS HOTEL

Via Urbana 6
Colosseum and
San Giovanni ⑤
+39 06 4891 3446
fifteenkeys.com

A former townhouse, remodelled into a modern and minimalistic boutique hotel with, you guessed it, just 15 stylish rooms, a charming inner courtyard and a bar that often hosts live jazz music at night. If you're feeling particularly adventurous, there are bikes available for guests to explore the city.

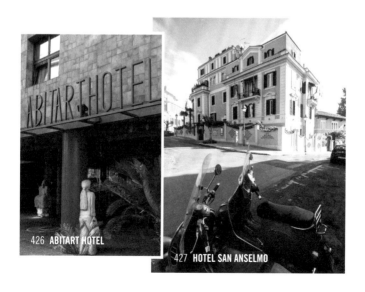

426 ABITART HOTEL

427 HOTEL SAN ANSELMO

5 fine
DESIGN HOTELS

431 **D.O.M HOTEL**

Via Giulia 131
Centre West ③
+39 06 683 2144
domhotelroma.com

Converted from a 17th-century palazzo,
D.O.M projects an atmosphere of fine
Scotch and Nick Cave music. Maybe it
has to do with the crystal chandeliers,
suede furniture and the deer skulls on the
exposed-brick walls. The tastefully plush
rooms earn this hotel's five stars, especially
the suite with the private terrace.

432 **PORTRAIT ROMA**

Via Bocca di Leone 23
Trident ④
+39 06 6938 0742
lungarnocollection.com

Its location above the Ferragamo store
in the high-end Via Condotti is your first
clue about Portrait Roma. You'll never
see the Ferragamo logo, just the panache,
with its classic-contemporary decor by
famed interior designer Michele Bonan.
The terrace is one of the best around the
Spanish Steps.

433 **G-ROUGH**

Piazza di Pasquino 69
Centre West ③
+39 06 6880 1085
g-rough.com

The 'rough' in the title could stand for
the exposed walls in this luxury hotel,
stripped as they are of any paint or
decoration. That coldness is balanced with
the warm colours in the velvet furniture,
and exposed wooden ceilings. The vibe is
shabby-chic, and urban hipster.

434 **HOTEL RIPA ROMA**

Via degli Orti
di Trastevere 3
Trastevere and
Gianicolo ⑦
+39 06 58 611
hotelriparoma.com

Hotel Ripa Roma is a large four star hotel that borders on futuristic. Its nearly 200 rooms come in six different varieties. Architecturally the most interesting are the loft-style executive rooms with a balcony, and the junior suites, with their Scandinavian furniture and vaulted ceilings.

435 **HOTEL DONNA CAMILLA SAVELLI**

Via Garibaldi 27
Trastevere and
Gianicolo ⑦
+39 06 588 861
hoteldonnacamilla
savelli.com

This beautifully designed hotel got a headstart in the 16th century. That's when Baroque master Francesco Borromini built it as a monastery. Today his tall archways and coffered ceiling make up 78 rooms. For outdoor space, there's a rooftop terrace and a flower garden in the cloister.

435 HOTEL DONNA CAMILLA SAVELLI

'THE DYING CITY' – CIVITA DI BAGNOREGIO

30 WEEKEND ACTIVITIES

---

5 of the best **DAY-TRIPS** from Rome —————— 228

5 **WEEKEND ESCAPES** outside of Rome ——— 231

5 **BIKE ROUTES, TOURS,**
and **PIT STOPS** ————————————————— 233

5 **SPORTS CENTRES** and **CLUBS** ————— 235

5 things to do and see **ALONG THE RIVER** —— 238

The 5 most **QUIET PLACES** to relax ————— 240

5 of the best
DAY-TRIPS
from Rome

---

436 FOSSANOVA ABBEY

Via San Tommaso
d'Aquino 1
Priverno
+39 0773 900 024
abbaziadifossanova.it

About 100 km Southeast of Rome, this Cistercian monastery is considered the archetype of the Burgundian Early Gothic style in Italy. The complex develops around a magnificent cloister, with the refectory and the monks' cells. The church naves are unadorned and austere yet very elegant, with pointed arches, high vaults, and rose windows. This is where the Dominican Thomas Aquinas died on March 7, 1274.

437 NINFA GARDEN

Via Provinciale
Ninfina 68
Cisterna di Latina
+39 0773 188 0888
giardinodininfa.eu

You'd think this huge garden had been photoshopped if you saw it as a screensaver. It gets its name from an ancient temple to the nymphs, and the river Nymphaeus, a natural spring that bubbles on its grounds. In the Middle Ages it was a thriving municipality. Today, it's a verdant ghost town, with plants and ivy growing on and around a castle, churches, and dwellings.

436 FOSSANOVA ABBEY

439 'THE DYING CITY' – CIVITA DI BAGNOREGIO

438 **CAPRAROLA**
comune.caprarola.vt.it

Caprarola is a Medieval village nestled in the volcanic Cimini hills north of Rome, home to the Renaissance Villa Caprarola, or Villa Farnese as it's also known, famous for its pentagonal floorplan, stunning hillside garden, and Mannerist frescoes that include detailed continental maps.

439 **'THE DYING CITY'**
– CIVITA DI BAGNOREGIO
infoviterbo.it/civita-di-bagnoregio

Perched atop a hill among the valleys formed by the Chiaro and Torbido rivers, the medieval town of Civita di Bagnoregio clings to the edge of a cliff. Much of the town's edges have crumbled as the foundation has eroded over the centuries, earning it the nickname 'the dying city'. Roughly a dozen people still live here. It's reachable only by an elevated footbridge.

440 **VULCI**
+39 0766 89298
vulci.it

This once prominent Etruscan city fell into obscurity with the rise of the Roman Empire. Then, in the 19th century, thousands of spectacular, ornate tombs were discovered, putting the site back on the map. Today you can visit the museum, and walk for hours around the ruins, which include the Ponte dell'Abbadia, a bridge with Etruscan foundations that were built upon by the Romans, who incorporated an aqueduct.

5

WEEKEND ESCAPES

outside of Rome

---

441 HERMITAGE OF SAN BARTOLOMEO
AT: PARCO NAZIONALE DELLA MAJELLA
Roccamorice
+39 085 922 343
majambiente.it/consigli-di-viaggio/eremo-di-san-bartolomeo

This peaceful hermitage in the Abruzzo region, built into the side of a mountain, dates some time before the year 1000. To enter, you have to hike through for about 45 minutes, then descend the carved Holy Staircase, which pilgrims used to do on their knees. On the saint's day, August 25, pilgrims still carry out a procession from the hermitage.

442 ROCCA CALASCIO
+39 0862 930 132
roccacalascio.info

A striking mountain top fortress from the Middle Ages, the highest in all the Apennine mountains, inside The Gran Sasso and Monti della Laga National Park. Its thick stone structure, and dramatic profile across the skyline have made it a favourite for cinema, for such movies as *The American* with George Clooney.

443 CERVETERI
comune.cerveteri.rm.it

Close to Rome, Cerveteri is the easiest Etruscan site to reach. The Banditaccia Necropolis is a must-see for its complex of tombs. But don't overlook Cerveteri's old medieval centre, which bedazzled poets such as D.H. Lawrence.

444 OFFIDA
comune.offida.ap.it

This picturesque town off the Adriatic coast in the Marche region is famous for the Romanesque church of Santa Maria della Rocca, a hulking piece of brickwork overlooking ravines on one side, and the town on the other. The area is also known for its *vin santo*, fortified wine.

445 SPELLO
comune.spello.pg.it

While the throngs overwhelm nearby Assisi, smart travellers sneak into Spello, just across the Valle Umbra. Here the wine bars are full of locals, Italian is heard at the cafes, and the town benefits from the same natural beauty as its more famous neighbour, with idyllic stone houses crawling up Monte Subasio.

5

BIKE ROUTES, TOURS, and PIT STOPS

---

446 APPIA ANTICA
South Rome ⑭
parcoappiaantica.it

Automobile traffic is almost entirely prohibited here, making for an ideal bike ride for miles and miles among ancient stone tombs and maritime pines immersed in the Roman countryside. It's best to use a mountain bike, as much of its pavement is still ancient, made of massive cobbles.

447 VALLE AURELIA – SANTA MARIA DELLA PIETÀ
Aurelio ①
piste-ciclabili.com

A great urban bike ride with stretches through parks, this bike route starts just behind the Vatican at the Valle Aurelia bus stop, and zigzags its way north through switchbacks up to Monte Ciocci, giving you a great view of the city, before carrying on to Monte Mario and Santa Maria della Pietà, a former insane asylum.

448 RISERVA VALLE DELL'ANIENE
Tiburtino ⑪
piste-ciclabili.com/ itinerari/4041-roma- riserva-della-valle- dellaniene

A beautiful route along Rome's lesser-known river, the Aniene. The ride starts from Mammolo bridge, passing through lots of greenery, some of which is unpaved. For a small stretch, you pass through the woods and have to carry your bike. Note that Rom encampments are common around the Nomentana bridge.

449 FREE BIKE TOURS ROME

**Via delle Botteghe Oscure 35 / Piazza dei Calcarari 4
Centre West ③
+39 328 562 5201
*freebiketoursrome.com***

Rather than free, these bike tours operate on a 'pay what you want' basis, whereby you pay at the end of your tour what you think is fair. Clients meet their guide at one of the two meeting points, where they rent a bike for 10 euro. Rides last for about four hours, and can be entirely customised based on what you'd like to see, from the countryside of the Appian Way, to the urban revival of Centocelle.

450 SENZA FRENI CICLOFFICINE

**Via dei Leutari 30A/31
Centre West ③
+39 348 777 3530**

A great little bike shop just behind Piazza Navona. You can rent your two wheels for the day for about 10 euro. They work long hours, so you can start your day bright and early (8.30 am) and go as long and as far as your legs will take you (but they do close at 8 pm). They also restore and revamp old bikes.

446 APPIA ANTICA

5

SPORTS CENTRES
and CLUBS

---

451 COMPLESSO NATATORIO DEL FORO ITALICO

Piazza Lauro
de Bosis 3
Aurelio ⓘ
+39 06 3272 3315
*federnuoto.it/centri-
federali/c-f-complesso-
natatorio-foro-italico*

One of Italy's premier aquatics centres, the Complesso Natatorio del Foro Italico dates back to 1959 when it was built to host the swimming portion of the modern pentathlon of the 1960 Summer Olympics. It includes five pools, two of which are covered, offering various levels of swimming training.

451 COMPLESSO NATATORIO DEL FORO ITALICO

452 **CANOTTIERI NAVALIA**
Lungotevere
Arnaldo da Brescia
Centre North ⑨
+39 327 142 0728
canottierinavalia.com

A rowing club on the Tiber River that dates back to 1931, Canottieri Navalia is located upriver from the Vatican. The club is devoted to competitive rowing, but offers lessons for all ages and skill levels, even for tourists interested in this unique way of experiencing the city and its river ecosystem. Book ahead by phone.

452 CANOTTIERI NAVALIA

453 CENTRO SPORTIVO GIULIO ONESTI

Largo Giulio Onesti 1
Centre North ⑨
+39 06 3272 9323
onesti.coni.it

Centro Sportivo Giulio Onesti is an official training grounds for Italian Olympic athletes, covering over 25 hectares of indoor and outdoor sports facilities, including Italy's Institute of Sports Medicine and Science. It also rents its facilities and lodging to visiting athletes and teams from around the world.

454 CIRCOLO DEL GOLF DI ROMA

Via Appia
Nuova 716-A
South Rome ⑭
+39 06 780 3407
golfroma.it

Surrounded by cypress trees and maritime pines, these links date back to 1903, built to accommodate the needs of visiting British and American diplomats. It remained the only 18-hole golf course south of Florence for much of the 20th century. It also has a driving range, billiards room, and swimming pool.

455 ANTICA TORRE – CAVALIERI APPIA ANTICA

Via dei Cercenii 15
South Rome ⑭
+39 392 788 5168
ridingancientrome.it

This co-op of organic food cultivators also offers horseback riding off the Appian Way. Fan favourites include catered rides, where visitors stop along the way to have a picnic, made with their homegrown food. They also offer romantic sunset rides for couples. On a full moon, you can book a nighttime ride along this ancient funereal path.

5 things to do and see
ALONG THE RIVER

---

456 CLOACA MAXIMA
Lungotevere
Aventino
Centre West ③

The Cloaca Maxima is the world's oldest large-scale sewage system. It was first dug over 2000 years ago to drain the marshes, then to flush out waste of all kinds into the Tiber River. Its opening is visible on the north side of the Tiber from the Palatino bridge. If you descend to river level, be mindful of the homeless encampments.

457 EMPORIUM, PORTO FLUVIALE
Lungotevere
Testaccio 11
Testaccio and
Aventino ⑧

The first-century river port of Testaccio stretches for almost 155 metres along the left bank of the Tiber. But few people know it's there, thanks to a lack of signage. It's characterised by travertine pavement, leading to two rows of warehouses for goods from all over the Mediterranean. Call ahead for calendar of openings.

458 KAYAKING FROM CASTELLO TO ROME
+39 347 243 9715
discesadeltevere.org

An annual excursion whereby participants gather in the Umbrian city of Castello, 240 km upstream from Rome, before heading down the Tiber River by kayak or canoe, all the way back down to the city. The trek can take days – some even travel by foot, bike, or horseback.

459 ONDINA GENERALI

Lungotevere
delle Armi 44
Vatican ②
+39 389 434 0884
ondinagenerali.it

Padel is a cross between tennis and racquetball, played on a modified tennis court surrounded by glass and steel-mesh barriers that keep the ball in play. This high-speed sport exploded in popularity during Italy's COVID-19 lockdowns when contact sports like football were off-limits. Today there are close to 800 courts in Rome alone. This is just one of them, overlooking the Tiber River, which has a nice outdoor lounge bar.

460 READING DANTE ON SUNDAY MORNING

AT: LA CASA DI DANTE
Piazza Sidney
Sonnino 5
Trastevere and
Gianicolo ⑦
+39 06 8629 5256
casadidanteinroma.it

The author of the *Divine Comedy* never lived in La Casa di Dante. Instead, this fortress adopted that moniker in 1913, when the government turned it into a research centre for his work. It's been hosting exhibits and seminars ever since. Every Sunday at 11 am, researchers put on readings of excerpts from the *Inferno*, the *Purgatory*, and the *Paradise*.

456 CLOACA MAXIMA

The 5 most
QUIET PLACES
to relax

---

461 CLOISTER OF CHURCH OF SAN GIOVANNI BATTISTA DEI GENOVESI

Via Anicia 12
Trastevere and
Gianicolo ⑦
+39 06 581 2416
confraternita-sgbg.it

Upon entering the church of San Giovanni Battista dei Genovesi, look hard for a little door on the left. Through it awaits one of the loveliest, most peaceful cloisters in the whole city. Ancient Roman columns frame a medieval well, while the walls bear 17th-century frescoes. Shade abounds. The cloister is open on Tuesdays and Thursdays from 2 pm to 4 pm (winter) and from 3 pm to 6 pm (summer).

462 ORANGE GARDEN OF CASA DELLE LETTERATURE

Piazza dell'Orologio 3
Centre West ③
+39 06 4546 0581
www.biblioteche diroma.it

What about reading a book in an orange garden? Pretty relaxing, right? Located in the former Oratory of Saint Philip Neri designed by Bernini, the cloister has chairs and tables scattered within the citrus grove. Despite being in the heart of the historic city centre, its peacefulness will make you forget where you are.

463 'MICHELANGELO'S CLOISTER'

AT: MUSEO NAZIONALE
ROMANO - TERME
DI DIOCLEZIANO

**Viale Enrico
de Nicola 78
Colosseum and
San Giovanni** ⑤
+39 06 684 851 114
*museonazionale
romano.beni
culturali.it*

The cloister – attributed to Michelangelo,
who probably prepared the sketches
for it – is one of the biggest in Italy.
It's nestled in the complex annexed to
the baths of Diocletian and it counts
100 columns per branch, with ancient
sculptures interspersed in between.
A quiet corner, removed from the hectic
traffic of the city, complete with well
trimmed greenery.

464 CITTA' DELL'ALTRA ECONOMIA

**Largo Dino Frisullo
Testaccio and
Aventino** ⑧
+39 06 575 8272
*cittadellaltra
economia.org*

Take a stroll through this huge area,
once a slaughterhouse, now dedicated
to 'alternative economy' (social and
organic agriculture, fair trade, renewable
energy, sustainable architecture). Every
Sunday, from 9 am to sunset, you'll find
a farmers' market, while every day, except
on Mondays, you can go for a drink at the
cafe or stop at the children's bookstore.

465 FABRICA

**Via Girolamo
Savonarola 8
Vatican** ②
+39 06 3972 5514

Not far from the Vatican, this former
pastry shop, turned into tea house
and wine bar, is the perfect place for
a quiet afternoon, for reading a book
or chatting while sipping on a cup of tea
(they have over 80 blends, also for sale)
and savouring a slice of cake. At dinner
and for Sunday brunch it becomes
more chaotic.

OPTICAL ILLUSION IN GALLERIA SPADA

35 RANDOM FACTS AND USEFUL DETAILS

5 fascinating **BOOKS** about Rome ———————— 244

The 5 most useful **APPS** ———————— 246

5 tips to **NAVIGATE ROME** ———————— 248

5 **ROMANTIC PLACES** to charm ———————— 250

5 quirky **ROMAN SAYINGS** ———————— 253

5 cool **INSCRIPTIONS** ———————— 255

5 intriguing **OPTICAL ILLUSIONS** ———————— 258

5 fascinating
B O O K S
about Rome

---

466 THE POPE'S ELEPHANT
by Silvio Bedini

What do you think would be the appropriate pet for a pope? For King Manuel I of Portugal it was a white elephant, named Hanno, which he gave to Pope Leo X in 1514. Hanno only lived two years at the papal court, but he was a huge attraction, and paraded through the city on processions. He was buried in the Belvedere courtyard at the Vatican.

467 THE WOMAN OF ROME
by Alberto Moravia

Regarded as one of Moravia's most critically acclaimed books, it tells the story of a woman of humble origins, Adriana, who prostitutes herself to provide for her and her mother, and the intricate relationships that stem from it. Set during Fascism, it highlights such themes as moral decline, corruption, sex, power, social climbing, and the intrinsic contradictions of the human condition, while attacking bourgeois moral values.

468 SONNETS

by Giuseppe Gioachino Belli

Composed in Roman dialect, these 2279 sonnets focus mainly on two themes: critical parodies of everyday life in early 18th-century Rome, and fierce attacks on the powers that be, from the papacy to the aristocracy, from politicians to intellectuals, even peasants. This body of work was published posthumously, and was heavily censored. A complete edition came out only in 1988.

469 THE IMPERFECTIONISTS

by Tom Rachman

A novel set in modern Rome, following the private and professional lives of the staff of an English-language newspaper struggling to keep up with upheavals in the digitising media world, and their own lives. The author, who worked at the Associated Press's Rome bureau, knows what he speaks about.

470 THE RAGAZZI

by Pier Paolo Pasolini

A fictional account by Italy's most scandalous 20th-century writer about life in the post-war slums of Rome, played out by a gang of street kids surviving by their wits. Its bleak themes of betrayal, theft, and prostitution are common in Pasolini's films such as *Mama Roma*.

The 5 most useful
A P P S

471 MYCICERO
mycicero.it

A handy transportation app, with a variety of features. It allows you to pay only for the minutes used in a parking space. When planning a route, it lists the best means of transportation, and provides a link to the website, whether it's the train, bus or metro. It also lets you buy the tickets directly from the app itself – especially useful for the bus, when kiosks can be hard to find.

472 FREENOW
free-now.com/it/taxi-roma

Ride-sharing apps like Uber never took off in Italy thanks to powerful taxi-drivers' unions. Fortunately there's FreeNow to fill the void. This app helps you find licensed taxi-drivers that come to your doorstep. You can rate the quality of the driver and the car, which helps to prevent scamming.

473 ENJOY
enjoy.eni.com

Nothing says 'Italy' like a FIAT 500. Enjoy is a car sharing provider that uses a fleet of flaming red 500s. It's a great option if you want to rent a car for just a few hours, as you'll be charged by the minute.

474 MEDINACTION

medinaction.it

Romans aren't known for speaking English, and doctors here are no different. MedInAction is a medical service that will deliver a qualified, English-speaking doctor right to your doorstep, no matter the time of day. You choose when and where you want the doctor to come. You can also set up a video consultation. It's like the old days when doctors made house visits, only faster and easier.

475 I NASONI DI ROMA

In Rome, the public water fountains are called *nasoni* or 'big noses', because of the curved shape of the iron spigot. There are about 2500 in the whole city! This app will help you locate the closest one to you, where you can fill up your bottle with drinking water for free.

473 ENJOY

5 tips to
NAVIGATE ROME

476 4 MUSEUMS WITH 1 TICKET

+39 06 684 851
*museonazionale
romano.beni
culturali.it*

The National Roman Museum is split among four venues: Palazzo Massimo alle Terme, Terme di Diocleziano (Baths of Diocletian), Palazzo Altemps, and Crypta Balbi. Many will only visit one, if any. But with the same single ticket (7 euro if there are no special exhibits), you get access to all of them. The ticket is valid for three days. The collections in each site are extraordinary, yet largely unknown to the vast public.

477 FREE MUSEUM DAYS

Visiting Rome on the first Sunday of the month? You lucked out: that's when all national museums are free. But beware: certain sites like the Colosseum and the Roman Forum can max out early. The Galleria Borghese still charges a reservation fee. The promotion does not include city-run or private museums.

478 SKIP THE LINE AT THE VATICAN

m.museivaticani.va/ content/museivaticani- mobile/it.html

No, we're not talking about buying rip-off 'skip the line' tickets from street vendors. Instead, buy your tickets online from the Vatican Museum's official website, then skip the line and head straight to the entrance. Or, plan to visit in the afternoon. The ticket line is much shorter, especially on Tuesdays and Thursdays.

479 UBER DOESN'T REALLY WORK IN ITALY

The taxi driver union has successfully kept Uber out of Rome. The app still works here, but you'll only find chauffeured cars that cost more than a cab. Instead, download the MyTaxi app. It works just like Uber, but it uses licensed taxis. When you sign up, they give you a generous credit.

480 DRINK COFFEE STANDING AT THE COUNTER

It's all about the real estate. Rome cafes charge a premium for tables. If you sit down at one, your cappuccino can be more than triple the price at some touristy spots. But if you order and drink your espresso at the bar, it will almost certainly cost 1 euro or less. Sometimes there are high-top tables for free. Never be embarrassed to ask.

5
ROMANTIC PLACES
to charm

---

481 SKULL OF SAINT VALENTINE
AT: BASILICA DI SANTA
MARIA IN COSMEDIN
Piazza della Bocca
della Verità 18
Testaccio and
Aventino ⑧
+39 06 678 7759

There is no eros without thanatos. Tucked away in a class reliquary in the tiny basilica of Santa Maria in Cosmedin lies the skull of San Valentino, the patron saint of lovers. At least that's how the story goes. There are at least ten known churches in the world claiming to have his remains. At least this 8th-century church is worth the visit.

482 ENOTECA LA TORRE
Lungotevere
delle Armi 22
Vatican ②
+39 06 4566 8304
*enoteca
latorreroma.com*

This opulent *enoteca* is located inside Villa Laetitia, which was decorated by the Fendi family, who has owned it for centuries. The walls of the interior are adorned with bas reliefs of chubby putti, with columns made of pink Verona marble. Dinners on Victorian tables with orchid floral arrangements always include candlelight. Dress code: no shorts and no sandals.

482 ENOTECA LA TORRE

483 CUGINO

AT: THE HOXTON ROME
Largo Benedetto
Marcello 220
Centre North ⑨
+39 06 9450 2713
thehoxton.com/rome/
cugino-restaurant

When you're looking for a fun, yet elegant aperitif, this is the place. You can either sit at the outdoor tables in the garden or in the hotel lobby, which exudes cool vibes and has a vintage feel. They often have intriguing initiatives, such as Taco Tuesday during the summer or Natural Wine Wednesday (buy one glass, get one free).

484 FONTANA DELLA CARLOTTA

Piazza Ricoldo
da Montecroce /
Via Angelo Orsucci
South Rome ⑭

According to tradition, this fountain, designed in the 1930s by the architect Innocenzo Sabbatini, represents the symbol of the Garbatella neighbourhood, the kind and beautiful hostess Carlotta. Together with the nearby 'lovers' staircase' leading up to Piazza Sapeto, this was where couples would meet during the war and post-war period.

485 VIEW AT DUSK OF THE ROMAN FORUM

FROM: VIA DEL
CAMPIDOGLIO /
VIA MONTE TARPEO
Colosseum and
San Giovanni ⑤

At the top of Capitoline Hill, in the Piazza del Campidoglio, walk away from the statue of Marcus Aurelius on horseback towards the right, and you'll find this short, narrow road wedged between municipal buildings, like the mayor's office. At sunset, the light from behind you turns the Roman Forum gold.

5 quirky
ROMAN SAYINGS

486 MADE THIRTY, WE SHOULD MAKE THIRTY-ONE

Fatto trenta, facciamo 31. Attributed to pope Leo X, the saying refers to the consistory of July 1st, 1517, when he appointed 30 new cardinals. However, having realised that he had left out one important prelate, he immediately added his name to the list. Sometimes, when you've already gone above and beyond, it only takes an extra little effort to reach additional benefits.

487 THERE'S NO TRIPE FOR CATS

Non c'e' trippa per gatti. When you keep asking for something, but there's no hope whatsoever you will receive it, this is what a Roman may console you with. It refers to an anecdote from the early 1900s, when Rome's newly elected mayor, Ernesto Nathan, reviewing the balance, crossed out one item in it: offal for the cats that were used to keep the Capitoline archives and offices clear of rats.

488 DO AS THE ANCIENTS DID...

Fare come gli antichi … who chopped down the fig tree to collect the figs (or who ate the skins and threw away the figs), the riddle goes. It's used in those occasions in which your ways are very direct, to the point of being detrimental, or when you're doing something contrary to the norm and nonsensical, which can become counterproductive.

489 TO PAY 'ROMAN STYLE'

Pagare alla romana. A style of payment at restaurants with parties of two or more people. Instead of each person paying for what they ordered, the bill is divided by the number of people, then each person pays the same amount. If you're with Romans, you can assume this is how they'll pay. In which case, it doesn't pay to nibble.

490 WHEN A POPE DIES, WE'LL APPOINT ANOTHER ONE

Morto un papa, se ne fa un altro. An irreverent idiomatic expression that reminds us how nobody is indispensable, not even the pope. It's used in different contexts and applied to situations where we want to sarcastically remind our interlocutor that we're all equally replaceable, but especially with people who have a certain power.

5 cool
INSCRIPTIONS

491 OLDEST TIBER FLOOD PLAQUE

Via dell'Arco dei Banchi

Centre West ③

Originally placed in the portico of the church of Sts Celsus and Julian, it is considered the oldest plaque referring to the phenomenon of the Tiber floods. The date in the inscription is November 7, 1277, and the level of the water is marked by a line that cuts across the slab. However the real level is lost, as it was relative to its initial collocation.

492 SIGNED ANCIENT SCULPTURE

AT: MUSEO NAZIONALE ROMANO – PALAZZO MASSIMO

Largo Villa Peretti 2

Colosseum and San Giovanni ⑤

+39 06 480 201

museonazionale romano.beniculturali.it

In one of the rooms on the ground floor, on the left, the gorgeous 1st-century BC marble statue of Aphrodite as a Venus pudica bears the signature of the artist who made it. The inscription in Greek ἀπὸ τῆς / ἐν Τρῳάδι / Ἀφροδίτης / Μηνόφαντος / ἐποίε' reads 'work by Menophantos, after the Aphrodite in the Troad'.

492 SIGNED ANCIENT SCULPTURE

491 OLDEST TIBER FLOOD PLAQUE

493 PLAQUE FOR PASOLINI

Via Giacinto Carini 45
Trastevere and
Gianicolo ⑦

Dispersed throughout the city, there are many tributes to one of the sharpest and most controversial Italian intellectuals of the 20th century. This is where Pier Paolo Pasolini, who moved to Rome in 1950, lived from 1959 to 1963. Previously, one of his houses was in the nearby Via Fonteiana. The neighbourhood features prominently in the first chapters of his book *The Ragazzi*.

494 PLAQUE FOR APOLLINAIRE

Piazza Mastai 17
Trastevere and
Gianicolo ⑦

The plaque credits this area as the place where French poet and writer Guillaume Apollinaire was born in 1880, before it was completely renewed by the 1889 demolitions to build what today is Viale Trastevere. However, it seems like he was actually born in the Monti neighbourhood, in Via Milano 9, while the midwife was actually from Trastevere.

495 FOUL LANGUAGE

AT: SAN CLEMENTE
LOWER BASILICA
Via Labicana 95
Colosseum and
San Giovanni ⑤
+39 06 774 0021
basilica
sanclemente.com

'Pull harder, you sons of whores!' (*Fili de le pute, traite!*) Thus reads the Latin inscription on an 11th-century fresco in the lower basilica of San Clemente. It dates back to an episode in ancient Rome, when the prefect Sissinius ordered his servants to seize Saint Clement, but roped a column by mistake.

5 intriguing
OPTICAL ILLUSIONS

496 **ST. PETER'S DOME**
Via Nicolò
Piccolomini
Trastevere and
Gianicolo ⑦

Head to this quiet residential neighbour-hood for an astonishing panorama of the city and an incredible trick: at the end of this 300-metre-long straight road, you'll see St. Peter's dome. As you get closer to it, it'll look smaller, while it'll seem bigger as you distance yourself from it. The effect is even more visible if you're on a scooter or in a car and drive slowly.

497 **THE COLONNADE**
Piazza San Pietro
Vatican ②

Among St. Peter's many wonders is the red granite obelisk in the centre of the square. Near its base is a marble stone marker that says, *centro del colonnato.* Stand there, now feast your eyes on Bernini's colonnade. All of the columns have come into alignment, as if instead of four rows there was only one.

498 THE CUPOLA OF THE CHURCH OF SAINT IGNATIUS OF LOYOLA

Via del Caravita 8-A
Centre West ③
+39 06 679 4406
santignazio.gesuiti.it

Technical and financial problems made it impossible to build a cupola during the 17th-century construction of the Chiesa di Sant'Ignazio di Loyola. But few visitors in the succeeding centuries have ever noticed, thanks to the ingenious trompe l'oeil painting that simulates a three-dimensional dome on the flat ceiling.

499 GALLERIA SPADA

Piazza Capo
di Ferro 13
Centre West ③
+39 06 683 2409
galleriaspada.
beniculturali.it

After visiting the first floor, you're taken to the Secret Garden. There, a colonnade appears to extend over 36 metres, with a life-size sculpture at the end. In reality, it's just over 8 metres deep, and the sculpture less than 1 metre high – a perspectival hoax by Baroque master Francesco Borromini. Museum staff are happy to demonstrate. If you're there on the first Sunday of the month, be sure not to miss the sumptuous Piano Nobile, or Noble Floor.

500 ANAMORPHOSIS

AT: THE CONVENT
IN TRINITÀ DEI MONTI
Piazza della Trinità
dei Monti 3
Trident ④
+39 06 679 4179
trinitadeimonti.net

On the upper floor of the cloister, there's a corridor with two anamorphic paintings, i.e. images that come into view only from a specific angle. One is a kneeling Saint Francis of Paula praying under a tree. The other depicts John the Baptist writing the Book of Revelations. Open Tuesday and Sunday with booking.

INDEX

100% BIO 151
100celle Aperte 155
9Hotel Cesàri 219
Abitart Hotel 222
Accademia dei Lincei 125
Accademia di Scherma 131
Acquasanta 28
Acquolina Ristorante 64
Acrobax 155
Alain 114
Alberto Valentini –
    Ricerca 111
AlbumArte 175
Alcazar Live 81
All'Oro 64
Alternatives Gallery 106
Amphitheatrum
    Castrense 123
Anatomy Theatre of San
    Gallicano hospital 162
Ancient synagogue 169
Angelica 125
Antica Cartotecnica 94
Antica Farmacia 161
Antica Manifattura
    Cappelli 95
Antica Torre – Cavalieri
    Appia Antica 237
Appia Antica 233
Argot 77
Assemblea Testaccio 105
Aurelian Walls 215
Babbo's 85
Bancovino 79
Bandiera Franco 98
Bar Brunori Caffè
    e Vinile 96
Bar dei Brutti 82
Barberini Mithraeum 163

Barley Wine 75
Basement Roma 175
Basilica dei Santi
    Quattro Coronati 212
Basilica di
    San Bartolomeo 215
Basilica di
    San Crisogono 164
Basilica di San
    Giovanni Bosco 195
Basilica di Santa
    Maria Maggiore 160, 213
Basilica di
    Santa Prassede 183
Basilica di
    Santa Pudenziana 183
Basilica di Santi
    Nereo e Achilleo 133
Basilica di Santo Stefano
    Rotondo al Celio 179
Bauhaus Rome 59
Bibliothè 40
BiblioTèq Tea Shop 70
Binario4 114
Bio Hotel Raphaël 218
Bioparco 210
Biopolis Caffè 40
Birra+ 74
Bisteak 31
Bistrot64 61
Blå Kongo 34
Bomba 112
Bosco Parrasio 148
British Embassy 126
Caffè delle Arti 41
Cagne Sciolte 155
Calzoleria Petrocchi 95
Campisi 29
Campo Testaccio 157

Campomarzio70 111
Canapa Caffè 85
Candle Store 105
Canottieri Navalia 236
Caprarola 230
Caracalla's Baths 212
Carpaccio 30
Casa Balla 184
Casa Bleve 64
Casa del Cinema 198
Casa del Jazz 196
Casa delle Letterature 240
Casa di Santa
    Francesca Romana 221
Casa Manfredi 66
Casa Museo
    Alberto Moravia 185
Casa Museo Mario Praz 185
Casacau 223
Casanata 124
Casetta Rossa 154
Casette di Campagna 205
Casino dell'Aurora
    Pallavicini 120
Casino Massimo
    Lancellotti 180
Castel Sant'Angelo 142
Centro Habitat
    Mediterraneo Lipu 211
Centro Sportivo
    Giulio Onesti 237
Cerveteri 231
Chiesa del Santo
    Volto di Gesù 126
Chiesa di San Pietro
    in Montorio 215
Chiesa di San Saba 133
Chiesa di Santa
    Caterina Martire 168

Chiesa di Santa
Dorotea 194
Chiostro del Bramante
Accommodation 220
Chorus Café 90
Ciclostazione Frattini 204
Cinebimbicittà 208
Cinema dei Piccoli 199
Cinema Nuovo Olimpia 199
Cinema Nuovo Sacher 198
Circolo Degli Illuminati 80
Circolo del Golf
di Roma 237
Citta' dell'Altra
Economia 241
Civita di Bagnoregio 230
Clivio di Rocca Savella 139
Clivo di Scauro 138
Cloaca Maxima 238
Co.Ro. Jewels 106
Col Cavolo 38
Columbarium of
Pomponius Hylas 152
Come il Latte 45
Complesso del
Foro Italico 183
Complesso natatorio
del foro italico 235
Complex of Santo
Spirito in Sassia 162
Confetteria Moriondo
e Gariglio 58
Coppedè 142
Core Bistrot 91
Corno d'Africa 55
CSOA Forte Prenestino 154
Cugino 252
D.O.M Hotel 224
Dao 36
Dar Parucca 55
Del Giudice 113
Domitian's Stadium 213
Doppiozeroo 91
Dress Agency 109
Drink Kong 91
Drogheria Innocenzi 71

El Maìz – Venezuelan
Street Food 53
Ellington Club 196
Emporio delle Spezie 71
Emporium,
Porto Fluviale 238
Enoteca la Torre 250
Er Buchetto 50
Ercoli 1928 68
Ex Mira Lanza
Museum / M.A.G.R. 190
Explora 208
Fabrica 241
Faro – Luminari
del Caffè 86
Fax Factory 86
Ferro e Ghisa 30
Fincato – La Casa
del Habano 84
Finger 56
Fondazione
Gabriele Sandri 157
Fondazione Giuliani 175
Fondazione
Pastificio Cerere 174
Fontana della
Carlotta 252
Forno Campo de' Fiori 47
Forte Antenne 80
Fossanova abbey 228
Four Green Fields 156
G-Rough 224
Galleria Lorcan
O'Neill Roma 172
Galleria Spada 259
Gastromario 63
Gatsby Cafè 110
Gay Odin 58
Gelateria dei Gracchi 46
Gelateria Torcè 45
Giorgio de Chirico
Home Museum 184
Giufà Libreria Caffè 100
Gonfalone Oratory 180
Grande Moschea 168
Grandma Bistrot 27

Hermitage of
San Bartolomeo 231
Historical Museum
of the Liberation 165
Hopside 74
Horologium Augusti 143
Horti 14 218
Horti Sallustiani 121
Hotel Donna
Camilla Savelli 225
Hotel Majestic Roma 27
Hotel Palazzo
Manfredi 218
Hotel San Anselmo 222
Hotel Teatro Pace 222
Hua Yi Si 169
Hypogeum
of the Aurelii 153
I Carnivori 31
I Sofà 26
Il Baretto 90
Il Genovino d'Oro 70
Il Mare Libreria
Internazionale 100
Il Museo del Louvre 101
Il Vinaietto 82
Indipendenza 172
Insula of San Paolo
alla Regola 164
Ippokrates 34
iRooms 221
Jewish Cemetery 169
K Men Club 89
Kalapà 34
Keats-Shelley House 185
Kiko Sushi Bar 36
Knick Knack Yoda 49
Krishna 13 37
L'Allegretto Dischi 97
L'Antico Forno 62
L'edificio Postale
Roma Nomentano 131
L'OmbraLonga 83
La Bottega
del Soldatino 207
La Casa di Dante 239

La Chiave del Violino 99
La Chiesa del Dio Padre
    Misericordioso 127
La Fattorietta 210
La Formaggeria 69
La Gatta Mangiona 43
La Gourmandise 46
La Lanterna 126
La Mescita Monteverde 78
La Santeria
    Pizzicheria – Bistrot 49
La Sapienza University 131
La Soffitta Renovatio 54
La Stanza della Musica 98
La Tavernaccia 32
La Terrazza 42
La Tradizione 68
Lamps 60 115
Lanificio 196
Largo Venue 81
Latteria Garbatella 42
Le Altre Farine
    del Mulino 53
Le Levain 63
Lettere Caffè 82
Libreria Fahrenheit 451 101
Libreria Tub 88
Liuteria Americana 99
Livello 1 28
Lo'Steria 51
Luigi Pirandello's
    studio 185
Ma che siete venuti a fà 75
Machete Barber Shop 110
Mad Hop 74
Mademoiselle Vintage 108
Mama's Home Rome 219
Mamalì 206
Maria Sabina
    Wild Spirits 76
Marigold 27
Marmo 197
Marzapane 65
Massimo Maria Melis 107
Mausoleum of
    Santa Costanza 133

Mausoleum of the
    Ardeatine quarries 165
Maybu – Margaritas
    y Burritos 35
MAXXI 127
Mercatino del
    Borghetto Flaminio 103
Mercato dei Fiori 102
Mercato Metronio 103
Mercato Nomentano 103
Métissage Atelier 112
Mia Home
    Design Gallery 104
MIAC 194
Miliarium Aureum 158
Millerecords 97
Molo 10 29
Momart Cafè 26
Mondi 66
Monte Mario 138
Mordi & Vai 50
Mostò 78
Mr. Manzo 31
Muccassassina 89
Multisala Barberini 199
Museo Carlo Bilotti 178
Museo della
    Civiltà Romana 194
Museo della
    Memoria Giocosa 209
Museo di Scultura Antica
    Giovanni Barracco 176
Museo Leonardo da
    Vinci Experience 208
Museo MAAM 193
Museo Napoleonico 178
Museo Nazionale
    dell'Alto Medioevo 181
Museo Nazionale
    Romano 187, 213, 241, 255
Museo Pietro Canonica 178
Museum of the
    History of Medicine 161
Mussolini's Balcony 167
My Bar 88
Natinudi 206

Nero Vaniglia 87
Ninfa Garden 228
Nomas Foundation 173
Numa al Circo 204
Nuovo Cinema Palazzo 197
Offida 232
Ondina Generali 239
Ops! 40
Osteria Bonelli 52
Osteria Palmira 52
Ostiense Train Station 181
Otaleg! 45
Otherwise Bookshop 100
Palazzo Altemps 179
Palazzo Colonna 214
Palazzo della
    Cancelleria 118
Palazzo delle Poste 130
Palazzo Falconieri 140
Palazzo Massimo
    alle Colonne 120
Palazzo
    Mattei di Giove 148
Palazzo Orsini Taverna 149
Palazzo Pamphilj 180
Palazzo Sacchetti 118
Palazzo Santacroce 149
Pandalì 53
Panificio Mosca 47
Panificio Passi 62
Paralumi Lar 94
Parco degli
    Acquedotti 210
Parco degli Scipioni 146
Parco della Caffarella 147
Parco Torre del Fiscale 147
Pasticceria Grué 66
Pasticceria
    Walter Musco 67
Pasticceria Regoli 67
Pati Jò 113
Per Me –
    Giulio Terrinoni 61
Pergamino Caffè 87
Perlei – Gioielli
    Artigianali 106

Piazza Mazzini market 102
Piazza San Cosimato 151
Pinsere 56
Pirati Pub 205
Pizzarium 48
Pizzeria Teresina
  Senza Glutine 54
Piatto Romano 33
Pirò 29
Pope Joan 141
Poppe Party 89
Porta Alchemica 140
Porta Portese
  flea market 97
Porticus Aemilia 121
Portrait Roma 224
Poussin's tomb 152
Profumeria Parenti 112
ProLoco – DOL 68
Proloco Trastevere 44
Pyramid of Cestius 129
Quetzalcoatl
  Chocolatier 57
Rachele 206
Rashōmon Club 81
Ravioleria Esquilino 55
RE(f)USE 115
Retrobottega 59
Rhinoceros Entr'acte 61
Riserva Naturale
  dell'Insugherata 211
Riserva Valle
  dell'Aniene 233
Ristorante Chinappi 65
Ristorante Mekong 36
Rivendita Libri
  Cioccolata e Vino 57
Rocca Calascio 231
Roma Liuteria di
  Mathias Menanteau 98
Roma Shop 156
Roman Forum 252
Romeow Cat Bistrot 38
Roscioli Caffè
  Pasticceria 86
Sa Tanca Crostaceria 84

SAID dal 1923 57
Sala 1 175
Salumeria Volpetti 69
SambaMaki 35
San Giovanni Battista
  dei Genovesi 240
San Gregorio Magno
  al Celio 132
San Salvatore in Lauro 149
Sant'Onofrio
  al Gianicolo 132
Santa Maria degli
  Angeli e dei Martiri 143
Santa Prisca
  Mithraeum 164
Santi Sebastiano
  e Valentino 62
Santo Palato 32
Sartoria Scavelli 110
Scala Blu Vintage 108
Scenography 105
Schostal 94
Selli Food Store 70
Senza Freni
  Ciclofficine 234
Seu Pizza Illuminati 43
Sforno 43
Shakespeare & Co. 83
SiTenne 109
Società Geografica
  Italiana 124
Soho House Rome 221
Sottobosco 107
Spello 232
Spiazzo 44
Spirito 76
Supplizio 47
Sushisen 37
Tabaccheria
  Vannicelli dal 1954 85
Tanto Pè Magnà 51
Teatro Palladium 130
Temple of Aesculapius 161
The Barber Shop 76
The Beehive 220
The Corner 42

The Fifteen Keys Hotel 223
The Jerry Thomas
  Project 77
The Pantheon 160
The Scar of
  Roland's Sword 141
Theatre of Pompey 123
Tipi, Bar & Store 207
Tomb of Elio Callistio 152
Tram Depot 150
Tram Tram 51
Trapizzino 48
Trattoria da Cesare 32
Trattoria Perilli 33
Tre de Tutto 96
Treebar 150
Twice Vintage Shop 108
Under the Influence 114
Valle Aurelia 233
Vallicelliana 124
Via Livenza Hypogeum 163
Vigamus 209
Villa Aldobrandini 150
Villa Celimontana 146
Villa di Massenzio 177
Villa Glori 190
Villa Lante 128
Villa Maraini 129
Villa Massimo 128
Villa Medici 214
Villa of the Quintilii 128
Villa Papale
  della Magliana 129
Villa Sciarra 146
VinoRoma 79
Vinum Est 79
ViVi Bistrot 205
Von Buren
  Contemporary 172
Vulci 230
Worldhotel Ripa 225
Wunderkammern 173
YAKY 104
Zia Rosetta 49
Zuma Restaurant 41

COLOPHON

EDITING *and* COMPOSING — Luisa Grigoletto & Christopher Livesay
GRAPHIC DESIGN — Joke Gossé and doublebill.design
PHOTOGRAPHY — Roel Hendrickx — roelh.zenfolio.com
ADDITIONAL PHOTOGRAPHY — p. 67, 72, 77, 173, 209: Kathrin Ziegler — katziegler.com
COVER IMAGE — Complesso del Foro Italico (secret 345)

The addresses in this book have been selected after thorough independent research by the authors, in collaboration with Luster Publishing. The selection is solely based on personal evaluation of the business by the authors. Nothing in this book was published in exchange for payment or benefits of any kind.

D/2023/12.005/2
ISBN 978 94 6058 3315
NUR 512, 510

© 2017 Luster, Antwerp
Third edition, January 2023 – Third reprint, January 2023
lusterpublishing.com – THE500HIDDENSECRETS.COM
info@lusterpublishing.com

Printed in Italy by Printer Trento.

MIX
Paper | Supporting responsible forestry
FSC
www.fsc.org
FSC® C015829